AUSTRALIAN
ABORIGINAL RELIGION

FASCICLE ONE

INSTITUTE OF RELIGIOUS ICONOGRAPHY
STATE UNIVERSITY GRONINGEN

ICONOGRAPHY OF RELIGIONS

EDITED BY

Th. P. van Baaren, L. Leertouwer and H. Buning (*Secretary*)

SECTION V: AUSTRALIAN ABORIGINAL RELIGION

FASCICLE ONE

LEIDEN
E. J. BRILL
1974

AUSTRALIAN ABORIGINAL RELIGION

BY

RONALD M. BERNDT

FASCICLE ONE
INTRODUCTION; THE SOUTH-EASTERN REGION

With 45 Plates and 2 folding Maps

LEIDEN
E. J. BRILL
1974

This Section consists of four Fascicles

ISBN 90 04 03724 1

Copyright 1974 by E. J. Brill, Leiden, Netherlands

PRINTED IN THE NETHERLANDS

CONTENTS

READERS IN AUSTRALIA PLEASE NOTE:

This work is a serious anthropological study of Australian Aboriginal religion. It is designed to be read by adults, and is primarily for use in universities and/or similar institutions. It is not, therefore, for use in schools.

Where Australian Aborigines are concerned, and in areas where traditional Aboriginal religion is still significant, this book should be used only after consultation with local male religious leaders.

This restriction is important. It is imposed because the concept of what is secret, or may not be revealed to the uninitiated in Aboriginal religious belief and action, varies considerably throughout the Australian continent; and because the varying views of Aborigines in this respect must on all occasions be observed.

January 30th 1973   Ronald M. BERNDT

PREFACE

The present study of Australian Aboriginal religion is to some extent restricted in scope. The Institute of Religious Iconography approached me in October 1969 to write on this topic for inclusion in a series of fascicles to be published under the title of the Iconography of Religions. The Australian Aboriginal material had to fit into that pattern, at least to some extent, although the editors have been so kind as to permit a high degree of flexibility. One thing, though, was laid down initially and remained relatively firm. This was the focus on specific geographic areas. Expediency, and the logical sequence of the development of the material, naturally widened the range to cover most of the Australian continent—but even so, there are notable exceptions.

This is an introductory study: it covers only a fraction of the material available. Moreover, it concentrates on published data. Although a large amount of unpublished material has been collected over the years by myself and other Australianists, for obvious reasons this has not been included. It could well be that, when these data have been published, the more general statements I have made here will require modification or expansion. That aside, no overall study on Australian Aboriginal religion exists up to the present. Because of this, it has been necessary to approach the subject in the way I have done: it was an essential prerequisite before subsequent analysis could be made.

The material presented here is to some extent uneven. This is particularly the case in regard to South-Eastern Australia and Queensland. The reasons are twofold. One is that we are dealing with earlier published material which was neither systematically gathered nor especially detailed, and—additionally—is now subject to re-evaluation against 'live' data. Secondly, in regard to Queensland, and with specific reference to Cape York, I do not have first-hand 'control' over that area since I have not personally carried out field research there. The main body of this study is focused on North and Central Australia. There the situation is different: in addition to earlier reports, we are considering material which has been collected and assembled through the processes of professional research within recent years. It is also, to some extent, 'live' (that is, it is still relevant to living Aborigines) and can be anthropologically 'controlled' as I have varying first-hand experience with most of the socio-cultural areas dealt with.

Nevertheless, even within the Northern and Central areas, I have had to be selective. The material considered here is, initially, ethnographic and is presented in a summarized form. Within any one socio-cultural area, a vast amount of religious data is available; a large corpus of mythology and many hundreds of sacred songs which are dense with meaning and require contentual analysis, and ritual activity which is highly complex. Especially significant is the realm of symbolism, which is barely touched upon here. My approach has been to provide, in summary, a breakdown of major trends or emphases. Methodologically, this takes shape in the framework of the Aboriginal life cycle, examined as a mediating influence between man and his deities, and as part of the religious system. This approach has been determined by the nature of the material and by the general concept of what is called, in Aboriginal Australia, the Dreaming. It is determined also by what are regarded as primary foci in Aboriginal religion, which permeate the major religious manifestations. In other words, the way of treating the data is influenced by the religious concerns of Aboriginal man in the traditional scene.

Within that frame, theoretical problems are articulated, and become basic issues which may be explored more deeply within the total range of Aboriginal religion. Obviously there are further, more general and not specifically Aboriginal religious implications which could not be spelt out in this context.

A further practical problem has had to be faced. In the present climate of Aboriginal opinion, traditionally-oriented people in certain areas have been fluctuating in their views on the traditionally blurred boundaries between the secret-sacred, the ordinarily sacred and the mundane. Some are in favour of hardening or tightening these boundaries, and even extending them to enclose material that was formerly open and public. This is primarily a reaction against Australian-European intrusion, and an endeavour to sustain a religious way of life which is increasingly coming under pressure, not only from outside but also from within—from members of a younger generation who have been seduced by the attractions of 'something different'. In other regions, including north-eastern Arnhem Land, there is a contrary trend: several aspects of the secret-sacred (by no means all) have been more widely diffused socially in an attempt to expand active interest and wider participation in religious affairs.

Anthropologists are concerned with doing justice to the material available and presenting it in a fairly objective way, while at the same time adhering as far as possible to local Aboriginal attitudes in this respect. In this study, the material is assembled in such a way that it is designed not to do violence to Aboriginal views on matters of religious secrecy. For instance, it does not provide detailed descriptive accounts of ritual action, and it does not give indigenous textual sources. There is also the question of graphic illustration. The present fascicles cover a wide range of photographs of religious significance. It has therefore proved necessary to be selective. Many of the most secret-sacred aspects which could have been illustrated have been deliberately withheld, although the aspects to which they refer are noted, in summarized form, in the main text. Aboriginal societies were, traditionally, religious societies. If we are to achieve an anthropologically balanced view of Aboriginal life, the realm of the secret-sacred *vis-à-vis* religion in a broad sense cannot be sidetracked. While local opinion can be prejudiced in this respect, our major concern rests on understanding the total life situation of these people and, in doing so, presenting that view for future generations. Aboriginal life will not be harmed by the airing of such knowledge. On the contrary, it is more likely to be enhanced by a wider appreciation of its basic religious tenets. The factors destroying present-day Aboriginal religion are very much wider than scientific examination of it. This is not the place to discuss these; but they have to do with the very nature of alien impact, including governmental policies, which are specifically designed to adapt people of Aboriginal descent to the wider Australian society as rapidly as possible.

These fascicles belong to a series under the title of the Iconography of Religions. My approach to this has been as a social anthropologist. My primary concern has to do with the overall patterning of the various belief systems and concepts, and their expression in action: a focus on the themes which are held in common, along with variations on these.

I have preferred to see the iconographic dimension in socio-cultural perspective. I have, right through this study, referred to material representations and to symbols—but I have not viewed them in isolation from their context. In the illustrations attached to these fascicles, this pattern is maintained and they are seen in ritual terms or as part of their cultural background. To aid the reader who is primarily interested in iconography, a short section has been added to each Chapter covering the range of such material relevant to the areas dealt with.

Originally, the editors of the Iconography of Religions allowed me two fascicles, limited to a specific word-space. However, in the overall plan I had been following in my writing, its size in final rough draft was approximately twice that. After discussion with the editors, they very kindly permitted me to have four fascicles. To achieve conformity of size between the fascicles, it was necessary to change my own sequence of Chapters. Initially, following the Introduction, the sequence extended through North and Central Australia (including the western and eastern 'prongs' of the Desert) into the South-Eastern region, followed by the North-Eastern, and ending with a Conclusion. In the amended format, the South-Eastern and North-Eastern regions are followed by Northern and Central Australia, with the Northern area being divided into two sections. It has been necessary to have the Central Australian material follow the Northern because of the presence (in the empirical data, as in the analysis) of a 'transitional' area. More importantly, however, my initial logical sequence is retained in the Conclusion, and the reasons for this are set out clearly there.

Finally, I would like to acknowledge the debt I owe to the many contemporary anthropologists and others who have contributed to an understanding of Aboriginal religion in their own research areas. I hope that I have done justice to their material, and that my interpretation of it, against my own particular framework and my own understanding of the total situation, has provided a deeper appreciation of basic issues—both empirically and theoretically. The preliminary nature of this study will undoubtedly raise a number of contentious matters upon which argument could take place. In that respect, I see this as a positive benefit.

Secondly, my acknowledgement naturally goes to the very many Aborigines who have contributed to my first-hand knowledge and appreciation of their own particular religious perspectives. And lastly, but by no means least, I am deeply indebted to my wife, Dr. Catherine Berndt, who has patiently read through my manuscript draft and who has discussed this material with me in the light of her own research findings. This work was commenced toward the end of 1970, but constant interruptions and University commitments delayed its completion.

Department of Anthropology,   Ronald M. BERNDT
University of Western Australia
October 1971

CHAPTER ONE

INTRODUCTION

PREAMBLE

For a long time, Australian Aboriginal religion was not widely acknowledged as religion. Frazer (1933:55) claimed that 'among the aborigines of Australia ... magic is universally practised, whereas religion in the sense of propitiation or conciliation of the higher powers seems to be nearly unknown'. Early reports include many descriptions of rituals and ceremonies (called 'corroborees'), but hardly any references to their being religious—although, with the myths and beliefs supporting them, they were often noted as being superstitions (e.g. by Taplin, in Woods 1879). Where they were classified as 'religious', there was a tendency to identify them with Asian and European religions and to see them as 'watered down' or corrupt survivals (Mathew 1899: Chapters X and XI, provides examples of this), or as equivalent to what must have been, it was supposed, the beginnings of religious thought and action. Worsnop (1897: Chapter XII and p. 151), however, drew a distinction between what might be regarded as sacred ceremonies and those (called corroborees) held mainly for purposes of enjoyment. Most of the early examples on this topic were concerned primarily with recording information which falls roughly within this category, without stating that it is 'religious' in contrast to something else. This is clear in Howitt (1904), where religious material is grouped under (for example) initiation and mortuary practices. Spencer and Gillen (1938) came closer to focusing on a religious system. Although they do not use the term 'religious', they do write of 'traditions' and 'totemism', and the implication is that they are actually considering religious phenomena. For example, a storehouse for ritual objects is spoken of as being sacred (*ibid.*: 133), and in the *intichiuma* (Aranda 'increase' rites) the religious aspect is 'most clearly seen' (*ibid.* 211). C. Strehlow (1907-20) also emphasizes that totemism is a religious manifestation.

It was really Durkheim (1954: first published 1915) who recognized that Australian Aboriginal belief and ritual were of a 'profoundly religious character' (*ibid.*: 23). This is not the place for a critical assessment of his view that it was an *elementary* form of religion. He worked with what we now regard as extremely limited and inadequate sources, with data which had not been collected systematically by professionally trained anthropologists. Of course, such persons were not available in Australia when he wrote his basic work. The main point which can be made at this juncture is that Aboriginal religion, speaking of it simply and in general, is not 'primitive' or elementary. In spite of all the work which has been carried out and written up since the publication of Durkheim's classic study, his heritage has dogged anthropological studies on this topic. Evans-Pritchard (1965: 57-68) is a pertinent case. Although critical of Durkheim's approach, he has added little to our understanding of Australian religion.

Contemporary theorizing on Aboriginal religion rests heavily on Radcliffe-Brown (e.g., 1952: Chapters VI and VIII), who was himself heavily influenced by Durkheim. Radcliffe-Brown refers to 'the totemic religion of the Australian aborigines' (*ibid.*: 166). But one primary issue in his definition of religion was morality (*ibid.*: 171). Others (like W. Schmidt 1912, 1930) looked for an overall god or supreme deity. The analysis of Aboriginal religion has suffered at the hands of writers who have tried to apply to it a conceptual frame derived from the so-called 'great' religions. The 'lesser' ones do not necessarily fit within that frame. This is not simply a matter of wide spatial diffusion for 'world religions', with the 'little' religions being anchored locally. It was tied, in part, to a narrowly evolutionary perspective. Radcliffe-Brown, for instance, consistently thought of the Australian Aborigines as being one of 'the lower races' (*ibid.*: 171), and he was at pains to demonstrate that morality was relevant in that context as it was (presumably) in the 'higher religions' (*ibid.*: 172).

Durkheim's influence is weaker and more oblique in the work of one of his own countrymen—Lévi-Strauss who, among other things, has taken up the problem of totemism (1962). According to Poole (Introduction to 1969 *Penguin* ed.: 9), *that* problem is now 'laid to rest once and for all': 'If we talk about "totemism" any more, it will be in ignorance of Lévi-Strauss or in spite of him'. Of course, it is open to question whether Lévi-Strauss (or Poole) was really concerned with understanding the Australian Aboriginal phenomena usually called by that term. To discard the label 'totemism' does not necessarily do away with the concept, or the problem. The label is incidental. 'What is totemism?' and 'How are phenomena of this kind arranged and what do they mean?'—these are two sides of the one question: one answers the other, or could do so (*ibid.*: 14-15). However, Lévi-Strauss has been particularly selective in his use of empirical examples (see R. Berndt 1970*b*: 1040-68). Also, except for Elkin's work, he does not use recent or near-recent Aboriginal field studies on Aboriginal religion; nor does Poole in his Introduction (Lévi-Strauss 1969). Again, this is not the place to discuss Lévi-Strauss' methodological stand. It is mentioned here only since some of the material he uses falls within our sphere of interest. The real issue concerns the facts—what they are and how they can be ordered to present an adequate explanation. This must be accomplished without doing violence to those facts, but at the same time it must go beyond them in attempting to arrive at an overall socio-cultural relevance.

Studies of religion by modern Australian empiricists, who have mostly been concerned with theoretical issues as these have emerged from their research, began with Elkin (1933) and Warner (1937/58). Warner took up Durkheim's concept of the 'church' in relation to religious expression, and suggested that as far as the 'Murngin' were concerned this was also relevant to magic (*ibid.*: 9). From that point, the focus has been increasingly on viewing religion as part of the broader setting of social life, as a contemporary manifestation. Totemism, on the other hand, is seen as a label pointing to a particular symbolic relationship between Aboriginal persons and the non-empirical, variously defined and expressed. The whole is considered as being coordinated by a belief system which is articulated in different forms of action, ritual and otherwise. Analysis has, therefore, proceeded in sociological terms, in relation to the organization of socio-cultural activity. Religion, so viewed, is the mainspring of all Aboriginal living.

The anthropological fieldworker in Aboriginal Australia has scarcely been able to evade, even if he wanted to, the implications of the non-empirical for ordinary mundane life. Aboriginal societies, in the immediate past as in a few instances today, are 'tradition-oriented'. That is, the guide for the present and for the future is found in what has gone before: and tradition, in this context, is primarily religious tradition. It is the *sacred* past which is significant—not just the past *per se*.

General statements, as contrasted with local studies, are not as plentiful in the literature as one would expect. Apart from Elkin's studies, R. and C. Berndt (1964/68), W. E. H. Stanner (1956 in 1958, 1959-61, 1965), Worms (1963), H. Petri (1968) and Strehlow (1971a, b) have all written broadly. Especially in the work of Stanner (1959-61), an attempt has been made to analyse Aboriginal religion structurally, drawing extensively on Durkheim and Radcliffe-Brown but using empirical material from Port Keats (Northern Territory). Elkin, Berndt and Petri have mainly been concerned with categorizing religious phenomena and correlating these with socio-cultural life.

These introductory comments are intended to indicate only some of the interest in this field of Aboriginal religion. The two major stimulators have been Durkheim and, more recently, Lévi-Strauss. Both have left their mark on Australian Anthropology. However, Radcliffe-Brown was able to say of Durkheim in 1945 (1952: 166) that 'there are many points in his exposition which I find unacceptable'. Stanner (1959-61: 108) has the same misgivings.

Structural Components of Religious Belief and Action

At the time of first European settlement there were, according to one estimate, about 300,000 Aborigines, divided among 500 or so 'tribes' on the basis of linguistic and territorial affiliations. Individual Aboriginal languages were not mutually intelligible, but most Aborigines spoke at least one language or dialect in addition to their own. People did not, traditionally, move far out of their own territories, although members of adjacent groups came together on ceremonial and ritual occasions. Trading parties did not go far afield, and objects were passed along established routes from one group to another through recognized trading partners. Outside contact on a large scale did not commence until 1788, although occasional explorers in coastal regions met small parties of Aborigines. 'Macassan' (Indonesian) contact was sustained for some hundreds of years along the north coast, especially in northern Arnhem Land, and made a strong impression on the socio-cultural life of the people concerned (see R. and C. Berndt 1954). However, these influences do not seem to have spread very far inland, except in a diluted form, and did not appreciably affect indigenous religious systems.

In other words, the Australian Aborigines (the capital 'A' distinguishes them from other aborigines elsewhere) were cut away from the mainstreams of ideas current in other parts of the world. They were forced to rely on their own initiative, and the way they chose was to model their life on past experience, which had been tried and presumably found effective and satisfactory. This attitude was crystallized symbolically in the concept of the Dreaming (discussed below). However, Aboriginal life did not remain ossified. It is highly unlikely that the traditional rituals we shall describe in this volume remained unaltered over the centuries, or that even at the time of first contact they were the same as they had been in the dim past. Changes were inevitable, and most Aboriginal social systems made some provision for them. They allowed some scope for behavioural variation, innovation and individual interpretation. Nevertheless, the accent was on non-change, and the religious views of Aborigines make this quite plain. What we must, however, underline is that these Aborigines were not a 'Stone Age' people or palaeolithic survivals; nor were their culture and social organization. They were *homo sapiens*, modern man. It is true that they mostly went naked, or almost so, that they used stone tools, had a relatively narrow range of material objects, and hunted and collected food to sustain life. But these conditions as such do not arbitrarily place them on the lower rung of cultural development. Against this material and economic poverty is balanced a rich religious spectrum, consisting of myth, ritual, song, dance, music and emblemic representations, among other things.

All of the Australian Aborigines lived in close association with nature and depended absolutely on what the physical environment had to offer. This three-fold relationship —between man and man, between man and nature, and between man and gods/spirits/ supernatural beings—was significant in all Aboriginal societies and all their religious systems. The primary themes revolved round fertility (of human and natural species) and the life crises (especially focused on the concept of re-birth). Around these two themes has been woven an immense body of symbolic knowledge manifested mostly through ritual action. As regards fertility, the fundamental emphasis was on food and sex, which in some contexts were very closely identified. In some cases they were treated directly and frankly. In others they were wrapped in complex symbolic allusion, expressed in song-poems and in ritual objects, emblems, and so on. Of the life crises, the first—physical birth—did not receive the same ritual attention as physical puberty, or even physical death. Nevertheless, Aboriginal ritual in one form or another stressed 'life' and living. As Stanner (1965: 217) has put it: 'The whole religious corpus vibrated with an expressed aspiration for life, abundant life. Vitality, fertility and growth ... Aboriginal religion was probably one of the least material-minded, and most life-minded, of any of which we have knowledge'.

Although initiation, as we shall see, was symbolic of ritual death, it was even more a ritual and social re-birth, conferring upon a novice a new status and opening the way to a whole new world of religious thinking and acting. Initiation for males, particularly, really served as an introduction to a new discipline, an expansive and expanding area of knowledge, a new way of looking at things within the social, natural and supernatural environments. Of course, using the term 'new' in this context probably overemphasizes the element of transition, since there were usually pre-initiatory preparations. Uninitiated youths were aware to some extent of what was involved, even if personally they were temporarily excluded. It was, rather, the difference between the ignorance of childhood, and social acceptance as an adult or an emerging adult, along with a ratification of social and personal identity. Where physical death was concerned, the attendant mortuary ritual had little to do with the facts of organic dissolution. Through mourning, the bereaved relatives were able to express their feelings of sorrow and puzzlement, and at the same time help the dead person on his journey. Mortuary ritual was a validation of living. It was another transition rite, in that case for the deceased. More than that, it was a ratification of life for the living—a kind of reassurance.

Our concern in this study is with myth and ritual: with a systematized body of knowledge and belief, and its ritual expression. The term ritual suggests a sacred connotation, not necessarily a secret one: but it points to actions of a traditionally regularized kind having specific aims, manifest and/or latent. 'Ceremony', in contrast, implies ordinary non-sacred dancing and singing, predominantly for entertainment, relaxation and social effervescence.

However, the dividing line is often difficult to draw in Aboriginal Australia, since 'ceremonial' activities were often aim-directed or had implications in broader social terms. Usually, they were 'open' (attendance restrictions did not operate) and they were not specifically designed to achieve results—except immediate ends such as emotional and physical satisfaction on the part of participants. It is such ceremonies that have mostly been called 'corroborees'. A good example of how the term was used in the earlier literature is to be found in Flanagan (1888: 50-2).

The most important ritual manifestations in Aboriginal Australia were those concerned with initiation, revelation (that is, post-initiatory rites at which only postulants and not novices were present), fertility (for example, increase of various natural species and of man, and seasonal-renewal-rites), and death (that is, extended or delayed mortuary rites).

Other, secondary examples include meditation and contemplation (where groups of postulants would come together to sing, anoint and view sacred boards, stones and other objects, make or renew emblems, and discuss the formalities of and arrangements for forthcoming ritual), spiritual associations (through conception or birth, 'totemic' linkage, dreams, etc.), and rites of love magic intent. These last raise some important issues. Love 'magic' was an important adjunct of religious activity, often focused on fertility in general or specific terms. It was on occasion part of sacred ritual, and was substantiated by myths which were essentially similar to the great ones that sponsored the most important rituals. (See C. H. Berndt 1950, 1965, in relation to women's secret-sacred rites.) However, such love magic rites were not carried out only by women, and they were relevant to both sexes. They will not be considered in any detail in this study; nor will the question of the relationship between magic and religion, which has obscured so much discussion on this topic. The great religious cycles of Aboriginal Australia included much that could be regarded as magical, and it would perhaps not be too difficult to identify this, but any demarcation between magic and religion would be quite arbitrary. For general purposes, sorcery is excluded. At the same time, sorcery in some parts of Aboriginal Australia, was supported by the patronage of great spirit beings who were believed to have given to man this kind of knowledge and the power to perform it.

Throughout the continent, in spite of regional and local variations, there was a way of life that can be identified as being Australian Aboriginal in contrast to anything else. One element which has contributed to this is the spread of certain great religious cults. These will be mentioned later. Some are very widely distributed and are recognized as having an almost 'universalistic' appeal. *Cult* is an appropriate term for such rituals which spill over from one group or from one society into another, and are accepted there. However, it has been handled rather loosely in the literature (for example, 'cult lodge', 'cult life', and 'cult totemism': Elkin 1938/64), and so it is not possible to keep consistently to the more specific usage.

Two major variables, or clusters of variables, need to be kept in mind when considering Aboriginal religious manifestations. One hinges on seasonal and geographic differences throughout the continent. In essence, this is a contrast between the coast and the inland (or 'desert'), between the fertile and the relatively arid. The other hinges on differences in the dimension of social structure and organization (see R. and C. Berndt 1964/68: Chapters II and III). This impinges on the ritual level in two ways. One has to do with social organization. For instance, it may take the form of a division between persons who play an executive role—that is, those who by reason of descent and spiritual linkage are the owners of a particular myth-ritual sequence—and those who are simply general participants. This complementarity is sometimes expressed as a contrast between 'managers' and 'workers'. The roles are reversible where persons of comparable age-grading are concerned, and those who are directors in their own ritual sequences become participants or 'workers' when they are helping owners of other sequences. A complex network of interrelationships, phrased in terms of kinship and reciprocity, is the social underpinning of all of the principal sequences—because all involve the cooperation of a large number of people. Whether they extend over a period of a few days or weeks or months, it is necessary to plan ahead and to organize food supplies. Over and above this, there is the collection of raw materials that are required for making non-durable emblems and for body decoration.

The second kind of influence, relating to social structure, has not been adequately explored for all regions of Aboriginal Australia. It is possible that a particular social emphasis—whether it be on matriliny or patriliny, on a moiety system or on subsections, and so on—does have both direct and indirect influences on the cognate ritual structure. It has been suggested that dominant fertility cults are linked more closely with matri-centred organization—in contrast to the male-oriented rituals of the Desert and, especially, of the Aranda (T. G. H. Strehlow 1947) and the Wailbri (or Walbiri: Meggitt 1966). However, that thesis is not entirely convincing, since in overall spread the two kinds of descent-emphasis are more evenly weighted. Moreover, the interplay of male-female sexual symbolism is not necessarily in imbalance, mythically or ritually: and to focus on one at the expense of the other is arbitrary.

Leadership is a vital factor in all sacred ritual. Leaders (both men and women, in their different or complementary spheres) become so by virtue of descent and kin positioning within a particular group possessing or 'owning' a mytho-ritual segment. In other words, leadership is ascribed in every instance, except where special dream songs or rites are concerned—and even then, it depends on the ability of the person concerned and on his or her association with the dream spirits (which, again, may be relevant to him or her through descent).

So-called 'cult' rituals of the Western Desert are nearly always segmented, being 'cut up' among a number of leaders not all belonging to a specific 'tribe' or dialect unit and not necessarily known to one another. In these, a leader must have a spiritual (social-personal) linkage with beings belonging to his particular section of the myth-ritual complex. He must be, as it were, a living representative or manifestation of one of these spirit beings since only in that way, so it is believed, can the power inherent in them be transmitted and made effective. An elder who is a leader—and not all 'elders' *are* leaders—'owes his authority not simply to age but to his position in the religious structure, and to his own initiative and effort within that framework', and this authority is relevant to everyday life as well (R. Berndt 1965: 167-206). Meggitt (1962: 248) speaks of leadership in a different way. Regarding the Gadjari cult of the Wailbri (Walbiri), to which we refer later, he notes that 'Once a man was recognized as a Gadjari organizer ... he remained a leader of all such ceremonies in his community until he died or became senile. But, unless he was an unusually forceful man, his authority did not extend into secular affairs, even in his own community'. In the contrary view, where spiritual association is significant in religious leadership it is also significant in mundane affairs. Strehlow (1970) underlines this same point. For example, he says, Aranda local groups were distinguished 'by bearing the appellation of the most important totemic centre located in their ... area. The ceremonial chief of this totemic centre was not merely a kind of religious guardian of its rites, myths and songs: he was a person of very real secular authority as well in his own [local group] area. This secular authority derived inevitably from some of the religious functions exercised by him ...' The major point here is the importance of religious leaders and headmen. These men are the 'managers' of ritual and have authority over others to the extent of being able to direct them to participate actively in such situations. The potential for this authority is something with which a person is born, but it must be enhanced through religious concentration and commitment if it is to blossom into full leadership; and it is also dependent on personal qualities.

THE DREAMING

A basic concept in the whole of Aboriginal Australia was, in some cases still is, what has been called, in translation, 'the Dreaming'. Durkheim (1954: 247), interpreting the work of Spencer and Gillen, speaks of the Aranda equivalent (expressed in the term *alcheringa*) as being concerned with eternity—a period when 'fabulous beings are thought to have lived ... their souls live for ever; they are immortal'. Spencer and Gillen emphasize the mythological component. It is not clear from the literature, however, when the term 'Dreaming' was introduced for this particular concept. Elkin (1933: 11) articulated it in his discussion of Karadjeri totemism (Kimberley, Western Australia). In that area, *bugari* (the Karadjeri equivalent) referred to a 'totem' but also denoted 'the long-past time when culture heroes and totem-ancestors lived on earth, made its natural features and instituted tribal laws, customs and rites ... the same term has the significance of dreaming ... The ancient time of the heroes is the "dream-time", but not the passing dream of the night; rather it is the eternal dream-time of spiritual reality to which historical significance is attached'. Elkin contrasts an ordinary dream with 'the great "dreaming" of dream-time ... the age of the mighty heroes and ancestors, who indeed still exist. And so a person's totem links him to that period and gives him a share in it'. Radcliffe-Brown in 1945 (1952: 166-7) contrasted 'mythical beings' with 'ancestors'. He referred to the mythic or Dreaming period as the 'World Dawn', and the mythic characters as 'Dawn Beings'. Stanner (1956:514) uses the term Dreaming because Aborigines 'call it [this] in English'. 'Although ... the Dreaming conjures up the notion of a sacred, heroic time of the indefinitely remote past, such a time is also, in a sense, still part of the present'. The Dreaming is no Golden Age. It 'is many things in one'. Again (Stanner 1965: 214-15): 'two complementary emphases stood out in the doctrine of the Dream Time: the fixation or instituting of things in an enduring form, and the simultaneous endowment of all things—including man, and his condition of life— with their good and/or bad properties. The central meaning was clear. Men were to live always under that foundation'.

On this basis, the meaning of the concept can be spelt out. In the first place, Aborigines used various words to refer to it. We have already noted two. However, almost every social entity had or has its own, from the Western Desert *djugurba* to the 'Murngin' *wongar*. All referred to virtually the same set of circumstances and phenomena. Some of these terms can be translated simply as a 'dream': but they also, as Elkin noted, refer (in the appropriate context) to a much wider and to a more general range of issues. It is necessary to be careful here, because identification of these two (that is, the mythic view and ordinary dreams) can lead to misrepresentations. This is to be seen (for example) in the works of Róheim (1925, 1945) and Freud (1938). Where the Aboriginal word is also translated as a 'dream', it is usually linked with the wider concept relating to spiritual conception or birth totemism, or to some variant on that theme: for example, it may refer to repositories of unborn spirits as in parts of the Western Desert, or to 'spirit landings' as in north-eastern Arnhem Land. The spirit child which serves to make conception known or to animate a foetus is often revealed in a dream or vision, or through some special kind of experience. This is not always the case, although there is evidence to suggest that dreams are not entirely dissociated from mytho-ritual contexts. This aspect will not be explored here.

Generally, the concept of the Dreaming refers to a mythological period which had a beginning but has no foreseeable end. It does not so much point to a period when the world, as Aborigines know it, was created. Rather, it refers to the process of shaping that world, making it habitable, or humanized—that is, preparing it for the emergence of a human population. The mythic beings themselves were in either human or animal form: mostly they were shape-changing. Many of them were self-created and creative, possessed of special powers which they could bring to bear on nature and on man, for good or for harm. They were not 'heroes'—although the term has been used in relation to them. Some were credited with having established a particular social order, and with instituting certain customs. In this sense, they can properly be regarded as 'ancestral'. More narrowly, the term applies to the great beings believed to have been responsible for creating human life, including the progenitors of contemporary Aborigines. Also, although they were allocated to the beginning of things, it is misleading to call them 'Dawn Men', if only because they continued to exist in spiritual form. It is true that in their transformation from tangible, mobile characters to spirit characters more or less anchored to specific sites, they retained the essential qualities they initially possessed. But 'dawn' suggests the past only, whereas these beings are believed to be just as much *alive* today as they ever were and as they will continue to be. They are eternal. In the great mythic epics and in the smaller tales, they performed acts and had certain adventures which will not be repeated: some were killed, or disappeared beyond the tribal boundaries of the story-tellers into unknown territories, or were metamorphosed as topographic features, or manifested through ritual objects. But such events did not alter their essential quality; their power was not diminished; they continued to live on and exert their influence. In this context, mythological or sacred time is involved, existing alongside secular time but not identical with it. Aborigines recognize both kinds of time as equally 'real'—as applying in different, although overlapping, socio-cultural situations (see R. and C. Berndt 1964/68: 186-8).

In the Dreaming, mythic beings moved across the land within and beyond tribal or linguistically defined territories. This means that members of more than one tribe may, as already noted, share sections of a major myth sequence that is linked topographically to a relatively wide area. In the course of their travels, these characters left behind something of themselves, something of their spiritual essence. But they also left tangible expressions of that spiritual essence in the shape of some site or rocky outcrop, tree or waterhole, sand-ridge or ochre deposit, and so on. In areas where galleries of paintings are to be found, such characters are often regarded as having been responsible for them: for example, 'He left his image in paint'; or, he (or she) 'changed into that painting'. Because of this intimate association with the land, they are intrinsically *part* of it. From the Aborigines' point of view, the two (land and mythical characters) are inseparable. Almost everywhere, through-out the continent, '"tribal" territory is or was criss-crossed with a network of mythical tracks or "pathways" along which such beings are believed to have travelled' (R. Berndt 1970*a*: 6). Along such tracks contemporary Aborigines too move in their quest for food—following traditional patterns. Even in this mundane task, then, they virtually replicate the travels of the mythic beings. Further, the movements and the incidents in the life of these beings, *vis-à-vis* the land, are immortalized in song and myth as well as in ritual re-enactment.

These characters varied in form as well as in type. All held in common an aura of immor-tality; all were closely linked to the natural environment. Not all were equally important ritually. But all bore a special relationship to Aboriginal man, both in social and in personal terms: 'they are bound to man by ties of familiarity and great intimacy' (R. Berndt 1970*c*: 217).

TOTEMISM

Although it may not be useful to speak of totems as separate or separable entities, it is undeniable that a particular relationship existed between man and nature and that this was mediated through symbolic expressions. These constitute an empirical fact in so far as Aboriginal Australia is concerned. Central to this concept is the idea of the Dreaming, which has been discussed briefly. It is through the Dreaming as a coordinated system of belief and action that we can approach an understanding of what 'totems' mean, whether or not we wish to use that label.

Stanner suggests (1965: 224) that 'the problems of understanding Totemism are the problems of understanding any religion anywhere. But because a name, or a category of classification, became a rubric, those who copied it unthinkingly came to have a *pre*vision of what they saw, and the problems were supposed to be of other kinds'. A view of totemism within the perspective of the Dreaming is one focused on a crucial attribute of the mythic beings—that is, their shape-changing propensities. 'They are closely identified with some of the natural species or elements, or are manifested through particular creatures or elements. In this sense, their spirits live on in the mundane world' (R. Berndt 1970*c*: 217). A particu-lar shape-changing being can appear mythically as, for example, a kangaroo. If that is so, then all kangaroos are 'a reflection of that spirit, all contain its essential Dreaming essence. The spirit character concerned is perpetuated in its continued presence on earth, through them'. Not all spirit beings *are* shape-changing; not all 'totems' (so distinguished) are directly linked to or reflections of mythic beings. But even if there is not this one-to-one connection, what the mythic beings left on earth, in the creative era, is part of themselves.

Nevertheless, the relationship is not simply one which exists between the spirit being and a particular natural species, or an object. As Elkin (1938/64: 165) has put it, totemism 'is a view of nature and life, of the universe and man, which colours and influences the Aborigines' social groupings and mythologies, inspires their rituals and links them to the past. It unites them with nature's activities and species in a bond of mutual life-giving, and imparts confidence amidst the vicissitudes of life'. This could be said about the

Dreaming too: 'It spells out a relationship between man and nature, between man and the natural species, in which man is regarded as part of nature, not opposed to other parts of it but bound to them by strong emotional ties, a kind of empathy' (R. Berndt 1970*b*: 1041). 'Beliefs about such a direct linkage with the major mythical beings imply ... the belief that man is not fundamentally dissimilar to them—that both share a common life force which is sacred' (R. Berndt 1970*c*: 217). The intervening 'totem' or symbol, in animal or other form, provides a tangible expression of man's relationship to his deities. The symbol, expressed through the 'totem' as an agent, is not explicable in its own terms. It must be seen as being part of the broader setting of the Dreaming. This relationship between man and deity is dependent on a variable range of factors. 'An indestructible essence or life force continues, it is believed, uninterruptedly from the beginning of time, and is present today' (R. Berndt 1970*c*: 243-4).

On one hand, that life force or power is immanent in the presence of these mythic beings at particular sites, or in their mundane manifestations—through various cognate animal species, elements, objects, etc.; and it can be activated in specific circumstances for particular purposes, through the ritual actions of man. On the other hand, every person is believed to contain the same spiritual essence as the particular mythic being(s) with which he is most closely identified. He may even be regarded as a living manifestation of that being. Saying that a person bears such a spiritual imprint implies that it is obtained through descent and membership of a particular local group, or on the basis of place of conception or birth. That imprint may be validated through a physical mark or some such form of identification: or through a material representation (such as a sacred board or stone: the *tjurunga*, for instance). 'Man is identified through the myths, and identifies himself within them: indeed, his character as a person is derived from this source' (R. Berndt 1970*c*: 244).

Briefly, then, in Aboriginal Australia both 'totemism' and the Dreaming have to do with social-personal symbols that link man with the non-empirical world: establishing a firm foundation on which belief in the essential unity of man as part of his natural environment rests. 'Totems' are the symbolic trappings on which Aboriginal man has depended in all circumstances. Aboriginal societies were/are rooted in the Dreaming, and in this was found justification for and satisfaction in living. What the spirit beings did and do serves as a model for what goes on, not simply in the ritual sphere but in all aspects of everyday activity. Moreover, the Dreaming—and, projected through it, 'totemism'—provided answers to the problems facing Aboriginal man in a variety of traditional situations.

The Sphere of the Sacred

The Dreaming as a concept, then, is all-pervasive, and although it is concerned mostly with ritual expressions this does not mean that it ends there, on the sacred or the secret-sacred ground. This raises the issue of what we mean, and what Aborigines mean, by the 'sacred'.

In most regions of Aboriginal Australia there are vernacular words that can be translated as 'sacred' or 'tabu' or 'set apart'. In north-eastern Arnhem Land, for example, the commonest of these is *mareiin*: it refers to any rite or object, place, song or person that is separated out from ordinary life; other local words are *duju* (duyu) and *daal*. Among the

Aranda, *tjurunga* has virtually the same meaning (see T. G. H. Strehlow 1947: 84-6); so has *darugu* among the Walmadjeri and Gugadja of the southern Kimberleys (R. Berndt 1970c, 1972). This condition of being set apart usually involves rules governing admission or exclusion, and participation, with sanctions framed in terms of supernatural authority even if they are implemented by human agents. In regard to ritual performances and the verbal traditions that substantiate them, these rules are a significant part of the social scaffolding of religion. One of the stipulated criteria is age. Another, even more important, is sex. Throughout nearly all of Aboriginal Australia, with few exceptions (e.g. Bathurst and Melville Islands), the major religious rites were dominated by men. In this sphere of relations between the sexes, the main role of women was to serve as passive cooperators or submissive supporters, as against the more active participation of men, the senior executives.

The problem, then, is not simply one of distinguishing between sacred and mundane. Divisions within the area of the sacred are just as significant—as Durkheim himself noted.

In most cases, the Aboriginal words for 'sacred' imply some degree of secrecy; but they do not necessarily stipulate what is regarded as sacred in a more general sense. They have overtones that emphasize the secret-sacred end of the continuum, whereas sacredness is much more widely diffused—it 'spills out' or expands outward from the exclusiveness of the secret-sacred ritual ground. Sacredness is undoubtedly highly contagious. It does not end or begin on the secret-sacred ground—if only because that ground is set within a more general social context, involving all camp members. Rites performed by initiated men in their own domain must be seen in balance. Even at the purely ritual level, they are not self-contained or complete in themselves. They must be complemented by activities covering a much wider range—wider spatially, including the publicly open ground in and near the main camp, and also varying in form and content. For example, (i) women, separately or in concert, may perform ritual actions (singing, calling out, dancing, gesturing) at a distance from the men. Or (ii) they may collaborate with men in combined rites before or after the secret-sacred parts of a sequence. Or (iii) appropriate behaviour for men or women or both may consist in *refraining* from doing something—or doing it, whatever it is, in a distinctively un-ordinary way, such as observing tabus on certain foods, or on speech, or not speaking above a whisper, or using a special 'language' (usually, this means a special vocabulary).

In other words, although the focus may indeed be on male ritual activity on a secret-sacred ground, virtually everyone is involved in one way or another. To begin with, there is the socio-economic interdependence between the sexes which makes it possible to hold a large ritual sequence; and over and above this is the actual content of ritual (that is, what it has to say), which substantiates its relevance to all members of the particular groups associated with it.

Aboriginal societies were, traditionally, essentially sacred societies. The whole land was full of signs left by the mythic beings. Not only individual sites, but the land and all within it was sacred. 'Anything directly related to the concept of the Dreaming, or owing its origin or inspiration to the mythical beings who lived in the creative era, was *sacred*, irrespective of the importance of such spirit beings in ritual terms' (R. Berndt 1970a: 7-8). But in such a context, can we speak of the mundane? In one view, a continuum stretches from the secret-sacred to the mundane, and the mundane would include purely domestic, economic and technical activities. However, this is not especially satisfactory.

In the past, a ready-made dichotomy was thought to lie in the simple contrast between the ritual actions and participation of men and of women. This view was supported by citing attitudes expressed by males *vis-à-vis* females, and *vice versa*. Women were described as profane, and hence antithetical to all sacred things, and not merely to the secret-sacred. It was claimed that they had the power to negate and to invalidate the sacred—almost, an anti-sacred power. But such views were not congruent with the data available, and have been contested by a succession of writers (most notably by Kaberry 1939; C. Berndt 1965: Chapter 9). Warner (1937/58), following Durkheim but using 'Murngin' data, draws a fairly clear-cut line between the ritual-centred life of men, as sacred, and the contaminating or 'profane' influence of women. Subsequent interpretation of the same material has not supported Warner's thesis, not in that respect. Stanner (1959-61: Vol. XXXI: 107-10) has also criticized "the profane" category as put forward by Durkheim (1954: 40-1, 138-40, 299-309). This category is, of course, not to be entirely discarded, since it can be defined as the negative aspect of the sacred, as being another kind of sacredness—not non-sacred and certainly not mundane, but probably included within the sphere of the magical (particularly sorcery). Investigation of this would need to focus, as well, on acts regarded as desecrating things designated 'sacred' or 'secret-sacred': revelation of sacred knowledge to the uninitiated, the despoiling of a repository of sacred boards or a mythic site, and so on.

In Aboriginal Australia, 'the male and female principles in some contexts are mutually dangerous and mutually antagonistic' (Kaberry 1939: 277). Nevertheless, women are not profane in the accepted definition of this term: they do not treat sacred things irreverently; they do not belong outside the religious system of their people; they are not excluded from the sacred. They are excluded from sections of secret-sacred ritual controlled by men (see, e.g., R. and C. Berndt 1964/68: 214-16), but not from all aspects of it, nor on all occasions. Men are, in turn, excluded from secret-sacred matters controlled by women (C. Berndt 1950; 1965: 243-47, also 273-81). Women, on the whole, do not possess the same extensiveness of religious knowledge as do fully initiated men who have been involved in ritual affairs over a number of years. But in the sphere of male secret-sacred ritual, women play a significant although a submissive role, and it has already been mentioned that their cooperation is quite vital.

In many cases there are both 'outside' and 'inside' versions: a major mythic constellation is known generally, at least in outline, to all adults, but its detailed symbolic allusions as well as its ritual expression are confined to fully initiated men. Also, in relation to the male-female discourse in this respect, it is significant to note that where the mythic-ritual materials of men and women are structurally and contentually similar, the women's versions are not as a rule so elaborate or sharply focused although it is clear that both belong to the same religious tradition. One further point concerns differing emphases. In male ritual, femaleness and maleness are not seen as necessarily inimical but as complementary, although one may be stressed at the expense of the other. In some cases, it is almost as if women are physically excluded in order to be ritually included.

Profaneness is not a special attribute of women any more than of men. A profane action, on the part of persons of either sex, is one that upsets, interrupts or violates the accepted pattern or quality of a sacred situation. A sacrilegious act is a profane one, as already noted (and examples may be seen in R. Berndt 1965: 191-4).

In brief, then, the dimension of the sacred is substantially the same as the Dreaming.

The field of the 'secret-sacred' includes things, persons and actions, as well as knowledge (most notably segments of myths, songs, symbolic meanings and so on) that are especially sacred, regarded as being of crucial significance. But, as we have seen, not all of the sacred is secret. Aboriginal religion throughout the continent was, and is (where it survives), intimately associated with social living, with relations between the sexes, with the natural environment and with food-collecting and hunting.

MYTHOLOGY-RITUAL

In Australian Aboriginal societies, large repertoires of mythology were the rule. Each constituted an intricate patterning of the activities of mythic beings—some 'great' (that is, socially and ritually significant), others of secondary importance. Not all such myths were viewed as sacred. Even within the sacred category, mythical characters were often graded. In western Arnhem Land, for instance, a distinction is drawn between the creators and instigators of ritual on one hand and, on the other, *djang*, tied to specific sites (R. and C. Berndt 1970: Chapter 2).

In almost every region, more than one mythic being is, or was, recognized as particularly outstanding. In one sense, Aborigines were polytheistic: they recognized that nature was made up of different forces, expressed symbolically through mythic characters, and that the significance of any one of them could not necessarily be graded, in terms of priority, in relation to another. In north-eastern Arnhem Land, as we shall see, the Djanggawul (Djanggau) Sisters and Brother inspired the *dua* moiety *nara* rituals, while Laindjung-Banaidja were relevant to those of the *jiridja* moiety. Within each of these myth-constellations, other spirit beings appeared, along with their 'totemic' manifestations. In turn, within each moiety, various clan-dialectal units owned sections of each myth and their members were responsible for the rites that went with it. Other ritually-significant myth cycles were divided up in the same way. Structurally, many of them were similar, built around manifestations of the same or related mythic characters. The differences lay in their association with particular stretches of land (correlated with local group-clan territories), or in their environmental setting ('bush' or inland, coastal or 'seaside', etc.). Mostly, however, they constituted variations on common themes.

Apart from the Djanggawul and Laindjung-Banaidja, in north-eastern Arnhem Land, the Wawalag Sisters and the Yulunggul Python stand out in contrast to many others. In western Arnhem Land, major figures include Ngaljod (the Rainbow Snake), the Yirawadbad (poisonous Snake) and Nadulmi (large male Kangaroo) combination, Lumaluma (Whale), and the Nagugur father-son pair. But in the Western Desert, for example, the range of significant or outstanding mythic beings is considerably broadened: and the same is the case with the Aranda (T. G. H. Strehlow 1947). Among the Aranda (Strehlow 1965: 139-41), the land-based *njinanga* (see R. Berndt 1970*b*: 1046) made up of men related in terms of father-son, constituted a local group, each of which possessed at least one important ritual centre (*pmara kutata*). As Strehlow puts it: 'all the main personages in the myth of each [centre] were revealed in dramatic performances, every [centre] possessed its own ceremonial cycle, that is, a long series of secret dramatic acts in which all the supernatural personages figuring in the local sacred traditions were revealed to the men of that [local group] in whose area the [centre] was situated. For the performance of the complete cycle a special ceremonial festival had to be arranged' (involving members of other local groups possessing sections of that same myth). A character was not necessarily confined to a single site. For example (Strehlow 1947: 28-9): the 'body of the *tjilpa* [native cat] chief Malbangka is (or was) to be found ... in the form of a *tjurunga* in each one of the many caves which are to be found along the far-flung trail which he and his sons once travelled'.

This is quite typical too for Western Desert myth-ritual. There, as among the Aranda, the local descent group, patrilineally oriented, owns a particular part of a major myth-ritual sequence. Such myths or parts of myths are focused on specific sites immortalized by the characters who appear in them, often created by them or resulting from some actions carried out by them, or representing their metamorphosis. The sequences refer to the wanderings of those characters, and some cover hundreds of miles of country. The whole Western Desert is crossed by the tracks of mythic beings extending in every direction.

This kind of patterning is, or was, relevant for virtually the whole of Aboriginal Australia. A close linkage exists between the mythology and the country, between the wanderings of mythic beings and the ownership of these myth-ritual sequences by patrilineal local groups. There are, of course, variations. In Bathurst and Melville Islands, the concept of the secret-sacred *vis-à-vis* ritual action is not directly relevant, and this was probably true for parts of south-eastern Australia. Howitt (1904: 509-677) gives descriptions of initiation rituals, but only occasionally correlates them with mythology. However, for south-eastern Australia he notes the names of primary mythic beings—Daramulun, Baiamban, Baiami, etc. He suggested that these represented an 'All Father' concept (*ibid.*: 488-508). Strehlow (1947: 7-14), too, speaks of 'The Great Father', but in his case he is emphasizing father-son pairs which define relations within a patri-local group; and this is correlated with the 'Sire' and his sons in its relevant mythology (Strehlow 1965). It is highly likely that Howitt was focusing on primary or dominant mythic beings. In his 'Initiation ceremonies, Western Type' the association between myth and ritual is clearly drawn (Howitt 1904: 643-77, and in his appendix, p. 779). (See Chapter 2.)

This connection between myth and ritual is close and striking throughout Aboriginal Australia. As far as the earlier literature is concerned, it is perhaps best brought out in the studies of Spencer and Gillen and Carl Strehlow. Not all myth is expressed through ritual, and in fact for any one area only a fraction of it is. Nevertheless, all ritual normally has some kind of mythic substantiation—not necessarily as a one-to-one fit, but at least as a framework of relevances which provides an explanation in terms of final answers. Mythology, as we have said, concerns the travels and adventures of spirit beings, either alone or in conjunction with others. Shorn of their shape-changing and magical properties, such myths reflect a close approximation of the life of traditional Aboriginal man. This similarity is perhaps clearer in the Western Desert and in Central Australia, where 'the physical, social and cultural environments of mythic man virtually coincide with those relevant to traditional and present-day non-acculturated Aboriginal man ...' (R. Berndt 1970c: 243). This is not to say that myth presents a view of the world as it was or is. Myth, however, is a reflection—*some* sort of reflection—of reality, and this is especially so in regard to basic assumptions. Mythic beings in the creative era lived a life much of which is relevant to traditional Aboriginal man. Additionally, myth is a guide to action, a blueprint; it contains believed-in truths, of vital significance to human action and human welfare (R. and C. Berndt 1964/68: 199).

However, although it can be said that the quality of life as reflected through the mythology is more or less taken for granted and that the majority of people concerned, living in traditionally-oriented situations, can be relied on to follow the patterns of socio-cultural living as laid down in the creative era, an additional factor must also be taken into account. The mythic era was not a kind of 'Golden Age'. Frequently, mythic characters acted in ways that are not normally open to human beings (see R. and C. Berndt 1964/68: 249; T. G. H. Strehlow 1947: 38-42; Stanner 1965: 217-18; R. Berndt 1970c: 216-47). 'Specific social actions [noted in the myths] do not necessarily bring condemnation and approbation, punishment and reward ... It is sufficient that these human beings have before them a body of mythic information in which they believe, oriented in terms of a way of life that can be identified as being basically similar to their own, traditionally' (R. Berndt 1970c: 219). The mythic beings were law-breakers as well as law-makers. Large myth-ritual cycles incorporate an ethical system that presents the bad along with the good, the immoral with the moral—viewed as a natural condition of man and a natural condition of the mythic being themselves. Such systems are concerned 'with maintaining a sequence of events, including social actions and ideas, that have critical relevance to everyday life: and, more broadly, with sustaining the *complete* ethical universe created and established once and for all in the Eternal Dreaming by the mythical characters ... and this includes sustaining the immoral with the moral, as necessary conditions of life'.

Religious or sacred mythology in Aboriginal Australia is normally expressed in poetic song versions. The main narrative outline of a myth may be known to everyone while the ritual songs and their symbolism are secret-sacred. However, there are exceptions to this. The Wawalag cycle of north-eastern Arnhem Land has both 'inside' and 'outside' versions (see C. Berndt 1970)—those for ritual occasions and those sung in the main camp, publicly or in the non-restricted mortuary rites. In the Central and Desert areas this division is not so obvious. But generally speaking, the sacred versions of myths, in their song form, contain much more detail and are usually arranged to form a cycle or sequence of songs. The length and structure of these vary; and some contain 'song words' and sacred words which require separate translation and explanation. In contrast to the descriptive detail of many northern Arnhem Land songs, the staccato 'key word' structure of Desert and Central songs nearly always requires an elaboration in context. As noted, nearly all myths of a sacred nature are associated with specific sites, and with ritual objects. And they purport to explain why such rituals should be held, and how.

Myth and ritual are interdependent and mutually supporting. Myth is one way in which belief is transformed into action. Myths are explanatory vehicles. In them can be found final answers, sometimes couched quite straightforwardly as 'We do this because the Djanggawul [or Ngurunderi, or the Wadi Gudara, and so on] did it!'. 'They instructed us to do this and so we do it!' But behind these superficial explanations lie others which depend on the interpretation of mythic symbolism (see Stanner 1959-61: 110-20).

Ritual is concerned with maintaining a life that is considered to have commenced at the beginning of time—a life instituted and inspired by the great mythic characters. Through ritual acts, it is believed, postulants may get in touch with these beings, and in doing so ensure that their vital life-giving power (*dal* in north-eastern Arnhem Land; *maia* in the southern Kimberleys) is brought to bear on the affairs of men. In a ritual context, the focus is primarily on two aspects: on the natural increase and fructification of the countryside, and on spiritual renewal and stimulation—that is, on the material as well as on the spiritual sustenance of man. It has already been said that the emphasis is on life, even within the context of mortuary rituals. The major distinction is not so much between rituals concerned with increase and fertility and those concerned with the re-enactment of mythical events. These usually intergrade. Rather, it separates predominantly initiatory rituals from those which concentrate on revelation. Of course, in both cases, acceptance and/or rejection are involved, and potential postulants must be taught. There are various forms of initiation: for example, circumcision, subincision, cicatrization, and so on, in the case of boys and youths, and puberty rites for girls (R. and C. Berndt 1964/68: 136-57). The experiences of a novice are mainly passive: things are done to him or to her—such as physical operations, which underline the initial teaching process and which provide him (or her) with a new status and an entrée into the world of religion. In adult rituals, automatic acceptance is only part of the picture: what is important is gradual movement through a series of revelations, combined with learning, and including active participation which is always conditional on a man's position *vis-à-vis* the particular ritual sequence involved. In other words, it depends very much on specific group membership and on kin relationships—through being a 'possessor' or part-owner of a rite, or through indirect membership (as through, for example, a mother, mother's brother or some other pivotal relative).

Rituals can be classified also in terms of those who participate either actively or passively in them. First, there are those in which only men take part. These are virtually always of secret-sacred significance. Second, there are rituals in which men have an executive role but the sequences consist of a more or less balanced activity by men and women—although certain sections may be restricted to members of one sex, usually men. Many initiation rituals fall within this category, although female participation is not limited to these. Third, there are rituals in which men and women participate together, in the same place and at the same time. Again, this is relevant to some initiation rituals, and to sections of the large revelatory cult rituals when men emerge from the secret-sacred ground. It is also significant in mortuary rites (of a delayed variety), and at Bathurst and Melville Islands in, for example, the *kulama* rituals where no strict sex-based restrictions apply. Fourth, there are the secret rituals of women, in which no men participate. In all rituals, participants decorate themselves and use emblems which vary quite considerably in design and in use. Some of these will be mentioned in other parts of this volume, but the most important are the sacred boards, the flat slabs of wood or stone, or long variously shaped poles, incised and/or painted, which represent mythic beings and/or parts of their bodies, or aspects associated with them.

ICONOGRAPHY

The accepted definition of this term, iconography, has to do with images, or, by extension, with representations of deities and their associations. If this is transferred to an Australian Aboriginal context, the description needs to be widened to include not only major and minor mythic beings and spirit characters, who have been shaped or painted in naturalistic and stylized forms, but a very wide range of other emblemic and ritual objects, designs and so forth.

Durkheim (1954: 113, 122, 126-7) discussed the significance of the 'churinga' (*tjurunga*).

He noted that this object is an eminently sacred thing, that its sacred character is so great that it communicates itself to a specific locality. He also pointed out that it is the incised marking on the object that gives to it its sacred quality. This (the marking), he said, *represents* the totem or mythic being concerned. What has been said for the *tjurunga* is also relevant to virtually all representations of a sacred and/or secret-sacred nature, except that I would add to this the matter of 'shape'. In Aboriginal Australia, some kind of expression of a sacred being, in material form, is nearly always present at a ritual performance. Rarely do rituals take place without some tangible symbol being present. These vary in size, shape, design, meaning and in their symbolic and practical intent. But wherever they occur, they provide 'evidence' that a mythic being is presiding at that ritual: that is, the being concerned is believed to take possession of the material object.

The object concerned must be mythically relevant and in a form established originally in the Dreaming: for example, an object which a mythic being himself or herself has entered into or is manifested through, or is a symbol of that mythic fact. However, although Aborigines generally say, when referring to (for instance) a sacred wooden board, pole, post or emblem, that it *is* a particular being, further enquiry makes clear that it is regarded as one manifestation among others. Also, there are variations on this particular theme. An emblemic object may be part of a particular mythic being, or something which is associated with him or with her. A bullroarer may be said to be 'the voice of Mumuna', the Kunapipi Mother, or male or female organs. Or, again, as in the case of north-eastern Arnhem Land, with the Djanggawul, where sacred *rangga* poles are of life-giving significance, their power is derived from these creative beings. However, in this same area, the *rangga* of other mythic traditions either represent part of a mythic being or have associative 'totemic' relevance. This associative relevance is just as common as full-scale 'bodily' representations of mythic characters, if not more so. As has been noted, in the Desert or Central regions and in western Arnhem Land (among other places), mythic beings were shape-changing, and non-human attributes also represented or symbolized them. As Durkheim pointed out, the actual markings on such objects are quite crucial and serve to distinguish the character and associations of one particular mythic being in contrast to another. This is demonstrated in the wooden slabs or flat boards of varying length which, when not used as bullroarers, are regarded in a general sense as metamorphosed mythic beings or as vehicles for containing their spiritual manifestation. They are distinguished from one another, not by their shape which, apart from length, is relatively constant, but by their incised designs. The same is the case with the wooden and stone *tjurunga* of the Aranda. However, the designs are not necessarily symbolic of the being himself or herself; usually they are a topographic chart of that being's travels, an 'on the ground' view of his sacred site or of the country associated with him in the Dreaming era. It is this abstract view of land in relation to the mythic being concerned which identifies him: this is his *real* identification, although the board itself represents his 'physical' aspect. In other words, the country expresses his spiritual linkage, through his ties with it within the Dreaming. His spirit is there at his actual site, the place into which he went, at which he resides, or which he 'became' or 'turned into'. This idea is transferred to the board's design, and that is regarded as being *the same* as the mythic being himself. The country is sufficient to identify him, and no representation of his image is considered necessary. As we shall see, in spiritual conception, a mythic being enters (or is responsible for sending a spirit child to, or causing an intermediary to send it) a woman and animates the foetus—it brings life. In the case of the sacred board or *tjurunga*, the mythic being's spirit enters it through the design of his country, animates it, giving life and power to that board.

The best contemporary discussions of sacred boards are to be found in Strehlow (1964*a*: 44-59), McCarthy (1958*a*: 29, 52-4) and R. and C. Berndt (1964/68: 366-9), and in the earlier work of Spencer and Gillen (1938: 128-66). It should be noted that, although great emphasis has been placed on design as a way of identifying a mythic being, there are also examples of plain stones of varying shape representing mythic elements. Usually such stones are painted or anointed with grease and red-ochre. This does not contradict what has been said, since an unadorned and unmarked stone can be related to many mythical accounts of such beings at the end of their travels and adventures and during the Dreaming era, turning into some particular physiographic feature. This feature is not necessarily identified by its shape, although in some cases distinguishing markings may be left to signify the occurrence. It is important to consider that such a natural feature is itself iconographic.

However, more directly naturalistic or stylized representations were also common. Rock incisings and cave paintings abound where, in the local mythology, mythic beings have 'turned themselves into' these: 'they made themselves thus ...'; 'they left their physical presence' in that form, and with it part of their spirit, part of their real self, *and their image*. Over and above ground drawings, the actual shapes of secret-sacred ritual grounds serve an iconographic function: they represent attributes of a creative being, if not that being himself. Ritual postulants and others decorating their bodies and wearing emblems are regarded as being *like*, as representing, the sacred beings themselves or their actions, or associative aspects. Such postulants are recognized, in many Aboriginal areas, as possessing an essential sacred essence which, through conception and/or birth, makes them a part of a particular mythic being, as an extension of that being.

Actual representations of mythic and spirit beings vary. The most outstanding paintings are those from the Kimberleys and from western Arnhem Land. In the former, there are the Wondjina creators; in the latter, the wide range of mythic characters, *mimi* spirits, x-ray 'totemic' species, and so forth. (See Mountford 1956; McCarthy 1957, 1958*b*; R. Berndt, ed. 1964 and R. and C. Berndt 1964/68: 348-85.) Religious subjects are represented extensively in the bark painting art of western and eastern Arnhem Land. Mostly, these were used specifically for illustrating stories—sacred ones, among others. Secret-sacred paintings were set up on an initiation ground, in western Arnhem Land, and novices were told the meaning of each in turn; or they were stored away with sacred *rangga* emblems in north-eastern Arnhem Land and shown to initiates during the *ngurlmag* rituals. In eastern Arnhem Land, stylized human figures of mythic and spirit beings were sculptured in wood and used in certain religious rituals, when they were held during dancing, or served as posts. There were representations of the Wawalag Sisters, of Laindjung-Banaidja, of spirits of the dead, and of others (R. and C. Berndt 1948; R. Berndt 1948, 1962). Mortuary rites provided a setting, also, for images commemorating the deceased (R. and C. Berndt 1949). The painted and carved grave-posts of Bathurst and Melville Islands were larger and more spectacular, partly because they were always set up in groups, never singly; they also provided a focus and a setting for mortuary songs and dancing.

While the wood sculpture of Arnhem Land was almost unique, the representation of mythic beings in human and non-human form was generally common. There are the *tnatantja* poles of the Aranda, made on a basis of spears, saplings or sacred boards, bound together with bunches of grass and with hair girdles, decorated with blood and featherdown, sometimes hung with *tjurunga*. Examples of these are illustrated in Spencer and Gillen (1938), while Strehlow (1947: 23-5 *et seq.*) speaks of these poles as 'living creatures'; others were extensions of the relevant mythic beings. In south-eastern Australia, figures cut in trees or moulded in clay or mud were common in the *bora* and other associated initiation rituals. (See Howitt, 1904: figs. 31, 32, for illustrations of Daramulun.)

All ritual objects are visible evidence of the reality of the Dreaming and of the mythic characters in their varying manifestations, either in part or in whole, in human or other form, or in their associative aspects (with things they themselves created, used or produced, or with which they came in contact). They are the material vehicles or intermediaries through which power is sought and directed by contemporary Aborigines. More correctly, they are the receptacles for the mediation of life-giving elements—in birth or in death, and in their ritual equivalents: through them, life is sustained and maintained. In this study, iconographic aspects are not seen alone but within their socio-cultural context, as part of the total religious perspective of these Aborigines.

Aboriginal religion, then, is expressed through myth and ritual: both belong to the Dreaming and are, for the most part, interdependent, one providing a consistent set of beliefs for the other. They also have a direct bearing on social life. Religion is relevant to all members of an Aboriginal society. This general significance is not invalidated by the emphasis on secret-sacred ritual carried out by men or, for that matter, by women. It does seem that, as far as women are concerned, magico-religious expression is much more personally motivated: with men, it is much more socially diffused. But myths and rituals emphasize a particular relationship to the land and all within it: that relationship is usually social *and* personal. It is not something which is abstract and removed from the common experience of man.

Man is seen as being part of nature, and in harmony with it. Without that recognized harmony, semi-nomadic existence would have been very difficult indeed: it underlines the need for patience and an assurance that renewal is a basic factor of living.

Further, religion creates a buffer between man and nature; it provides an assurance that man is not entirely helpless, that he can where necessary intervene at least to some degree in order to influence the forces which impinge on him. And he does this through the spirit beings who serve as intermediaries. Between Aboriginal man and these intermediaries is a relationship of interdependence and even of identification. Such beings do not stand apart from man. The force of Aboriginal ritual rests, not on its esoteric symbolic patterning which can be interpreted only by the fully initiated, but on its relevance to man in providing a framework, a series of answers to the problems of everyday living, and purporting to control and cope with the unpredictable and transcendental. Social relations in religious action have a three-fold basis. First, there are relations between human beings themselves, with a strong emphasis on cooperation, since rituals cannot be performed without the interaction and aid of others. They call for participation by both men and women, and the situation must be such as to provide a viable economic basis for holding the ritual. In this connection, the division of labour between the sexes is a necessary condition. Secondly, there are the ties between human beings and the mythic characters themselves; they spell out special kinds of relationship, linking Aboriginal man with specific beings and in doing so creating a commitment to certain types of action. These social and personal associations are crucial and lead to the third relationship, which places Aboriginal man firmly within his natural environment, as part of it, and dependent on it for his survival.

BIBLIOGRAPHY

Berndt, C. H. 1950. *Women's Changing Ceremonies in Northern Australia.* L'Homme, I: Hermann, Paris.

Berndt, C. H. 1965. Women and the "Secret Life". In *Aboriginal Man in Australia* (R. M. and C. H. Berndt. eds.).

Berndt, C. H. 1970. Monsoon and Honey Wind. In *Échanges et Communications, mélanges offerts à Claude Lévi-Strauss* (J. Pouillon et P. Maranda, eds.): Mouton, La Hague.

Berndt, R. M. 1948. Badu, Islands of the Spirits, *Oceania*, Vol. XIX, No. 2.

Berndt, R. M. 1962. *An Adjustment Movement in Arnhem Land.* Cahiers de L'Homme: Mouton, Paris and La Hague.

Berndt, R. M. (ed.) 1964. *Australian Aboriginal Art*: Ure Smith, Sydney.

Berndt, R. M. 1965. Law and Order in Aboriginal Australia. In *Aboriginal Man in Australia* (R. M. and C. H. Berndt, eds.).

Berndt, R. M. (ed.) 1970. *Australian Aboriginal Anthropology*: University of Western Australia Press, Perth.

Berndt, R. M. 1970a. *The Sacred Site. The Western Arnhem Land Example.* Australian Aboriginal Studies No. 29, Social Anthropology Series No. 4.: Australian Institute of Aboriginal Studies, Canberra.

Berndt, R. M. 1970b. Two in One, and More in Two. In *Échanges et Communications, mélanges offerts à Claude Lévi-Strauss* (J. Pouillon and P. Maranda, eds.): Mouton, La Hague.

Berndt, R. M. 1970c. Traditional Morality as Expressed through the medium of an Australian Aboriginal Religion. In *Australian Aboriginal Anthropology* (R. M. Berndt, ed.).

Berndt, R. M. 1972. The Walmadjeri-Gugadja. In *Hunters and Gatherers Today* (M. G. Bicchieri, ed.): Holt, Rinehart and Winston, New York.

Berndt, R. M. and C. H. 1948. Sacred Figures of Ancestral Beings of Arnhem Land, *Oceania*, Vol. XVIII, No. 4.

Berndt, R. M. and C. H. 1949. Secular Figures of Northeastern Arnhem Land, *American Anthropologist*. Vol. 51, No. 2.

Berndt, R. M. and C. H. 1954. *Arnhem Land. Its History and Its People*: Cheshire, Melbourne.

Berndt, R. M. and C. H. 1964/68. *The World of the First Australians*: Ure Smith, Sydney.

Berndt, R. M. and C. H. eds. 1965. *Aboriginal Man in Australia*: Angus and Robertson, Sydney.

Berndt, R. M. and C. H. 1970. *Man, Land and Myth in North Australia: the Gunwinggu People*: Ure Smith, Sydney.

Durkheim, É. 1954. *The Elementary Forms of the Religious Life*: Allen and Unwin, London.

Elkin, A. P. 1933. *Studies in Australian Totemism.* Oceania Monographs, No. 2: Australian National Research Council, Sydney.

Elkin, A. P. 1938/64. *The Australian Aborigines*: Angus and Robertson, Sydney.

Elkin, A. P. 1969. Elements of Australian Aboriginal Philosophy, *Oceania*, Vol. XL, No. 2.

Evans-Pritchard, E. E. 1965. *Theories of Primitive Religion*: Clarendon Press, Oxford.

Flanagan, R. J. 1888. *The Aborigines of Australia*: Flanagan and Robertson, Sydney.

Frazer, J. G. 1933. *The Golden Bough*: abridged ed., Macmillan, London.

Freud, S. 1938. *Totem and Taboo*: Pelican Books, Harmondsworth.

Howitt, A. W. 1904. *The Native Tribes of South-East Australia*: Macmillan, London.

Kaberry, P. M. 1939. *Aboriginal Woman. Sacred and Profane*: Routledge, London.

Lévi-Strauss, C. 1962. *Totemism*: Beacon Press, Boston.

Lévi-Strauss, C. 1969. *Totemism.* Trans. R. Needham; introd. by R. C. Poole: Penguin, London.

Mathew, J. 1899. *Eaglehawk and Crow. A Study of the Australian Aborigines* ...: Nutt, London; Melville, Mullen and Slade, Melbourne.

McCarthy, F. D. 1958a. *Australian Aboriginal Decorative Art*: Australian Museum, Sydney.

McCarthy, F. D. 1958b. *Australian Aboriginal Rock Art*: Australian Museum, Sydney.

Meggitt, M. J. 1962. *Desert People*: Angus and Robertson, Sydney.

Meggitt, M. J. 1966. *Gadjari among the Walbiri Aborigines of Central Australia*. Oceania Monographs, No. 14: University of Sydney, Sydney.

Mountford, C. P. 1956. *Records of the American-Australian Scientific Expedition to Arnhem Land, Vol. 1, Art, Myth, and Symbolism*: Melbourne University Press, Melbourne.

Petri, H. 1968. Australische Eingeborenen-Religionen (Worms-Petri). In *Die Religionen der Südsee und Australiens* (H. Nevermann, E. A. Worms and H. Petri): W. Kohlhammer Verlag, Stuttgart.

Radcliffe-Brown, A. R. 1952. *Structure and Function in Primitive Society*: Cohen and West, London.

Róheim, G. 1925. *Australian Totemism*: Allen and Unwin, London.

Róheim, G. 1945. *The Eternal Ones of the Dream*: International Universities Press, New York.

Schmidt, W. 1912, 1930. *Der Ursprung der Gottesidee*. Vol. I and Vol. III: Münster.

Spencer, B. and F. J. Gillen. 1938. *The Native Tribes of Central Australia*: Macmillan, London.

Stanner, W. E. H. 1956. The Dreaming. In *Australian Signpost* (T. A. C. Hungerford, ed.): Cheshire, Melbourne. Reprinted in *Reader in Comparative Religion*: an anthropological approach (W. A. Lessa and E. Z. Vogt, eds.) 1958: Row, Peterson, Evanston, Illinois.

Stanner, W. E. H. 1959-61. On Aboriginal Religion, *Oceania*, Vol. XXX, Nos. 2 and 4; Vol. XXXI, Nos. 2 and 4; Vol. XXXII, No. 2.

Stanner, W. E. H. 1965. Religion, Totemism, and Symbolism. In *Aboriginal Man in Australia*. (R. M. and C. H. Berndt, eds.).

Strehlow, C. 1907-20. *Die Aranda-und-Loritja-Stämme in Zentral-Australien*: J. Baer, Frankfurt.

Strehlow, T. G. H. 1947. *Aranda Traditions*: Melbourne University Press, Melbourne.

Strehlow, T. G. H. 1964a. The Art of Circle, Line, and Square. In *Australian Aboriginal Art* (R. M. Berndt, ed.).

Strehlow, T. G. H. 1964b. Personal Monototemism in a Polytotemic Community. In *Festschrift für Ad. E. Jensen*: Klaus Renner Verlag, Munich.

Strehlow, T. G. H. 1965. Culture, Social Structure, and Environment in Aboriginal Central Australia. In *Aboriginal Man in Australia* (R. M. and C. H. Berndt, eds.).

Strehlow, T. G. H. 1970. Geography and the Totemic Landscape in Central Australia: a functional study. In *Australian Aboriginal Anthropology* (R. M. Berndt, ed.).

Strehlow, T. G. H. 1971a. Australia. In *Historia Religionum*. Handbook for the History of Religions (C. J. Bleeker and G. Widengren, eds.). Vol. II, Religions of the Present: E. J. Brill, Leiden.

Strehlow, T. G. H. 1971b. *Songs of Central Australia*: Angus and Robertson, Sydney.

Taplin, G. 1879. The Narrinyeri. In *The Native Tribes of South Australia* (J. D. Woods, ed.): Wigg, Adelaide.

Warner, W. L. 1937/58. *A Black Civilization*: Harper, New York and London.

Worms, E. 1963. Religion. In *Australian Aboriginal Studies*. A symposium of papers presented at the 1961 research conference (W. E. H. Stanner, convener: H. Sheils, ed.): Oxford University Press, Melbourne.

Worsnop, T. 1897. *The Prehistoric Arts, Manufactures, Works, Weapons, etc. of the Aborigines of Australia*: Government Printer, Adelaide.

Note to page 3 on general statements concerning Australian Aboriginal religion:

Mircea Eliade's papers on various aspects of Aboriginal religion have been assembled in *Australian Religions*, Cornell University Press, Ithaca, 1973. Although his approach is essentially different from mine, we are both concerned with understanding the meaning of Aboriginal religions.

CHAPTER TWO

THE SOUTH-EASTERN REGION

While an appreciable amount of traditional Aboriginal life still survives in a number of areas within the Australian continent, radical changes have taken place at all levels. (See, for example, R. Berndt 1963: 385-408.) Here we focus on the south-eastern sector of South Australia, Victoria and New South Wales.

Where traditional Aboriginal culture does survive here, it does so in the minds of older people, as a 'memory culture'. What is handed on is considerably modified and often distorted. In some parts of the region, nothing at all survives: only the *idea* of an Aboriginal background, obtained from external sources—from the news media, for example. For these people of Aboriginal descent, traditional life is some generations back and seems to have little relevance to today's living. The same is true for the south-western sector of Western Australia. In other words, for information on traditional religious patterns we must turn to the work of earlier writers. The range of material available from such sources is covered by Elkin (1963: 3-28).

In a few localities, however, some features have survived, and these have helped us to interpret the older material and to place it in perspective. Notably, this has been in the mid-north of South Australia and along the lower reaches of the River Murray and in western New South Wales. At the same time (and again with certain exceptions), the material available on religious matters generally is rather sparse, especially in terms of our specific enquiry. There is, however, a great deal of mytho-ritual data. A lot of this is unsystematically recorded and not well coordinated with the overall socio-cultural pattern. Intentionally, therefore, I have been selective and only major trends are discussed, rather than detailed ethnographic material to support these.

1. THE LAKE EYRE BASIN

The tribes centring on this area (in South Australia), especially the Dieri, exemplify a series of Aboriginal cultures which are now dead. Gason (1874), Howitt (1904), Siebert (1910), Horne and Aiston (1924), Fry (1937), Elkin (1931a and b; 1934) and Berndt (1953), among others, have all contributed to our knowledge of Dieri (and adjacent tribal) ethnography.

Entrée into religious life depended on two kinds of membership: in the *bindara* (patri-local clan; depending on descent); and in the *mardu* (matri-local clan), which applied only during a person's lifetime and could not be passed on. Each of these was associated with a myth-constellation, and was territorially based. This ritual division supports Lévi-Strauss's contentions relating to matrilineal and patrilineal clan totemism (1963: 54), except that the heritage from a person's mother was not solely physical but had a high degree of spiritual significance. For instance, a man, especially, played a considerable part not only in rites aimed at the maintenance of natural species, but also in rites that were assigned totemically to the local clan of his mother and mother's brother (Elkin 1934: 176). Elkin (1931b: 58-60) notes that a person did not eat the totem of his *mardu*, since it was regarded as his own flesh, as deriving from his mother. Regarding the *bindara*, 'ownership is shown by the fact that after the increase of the species consequent upon the performance of the rite, they [the members of the relevant *bindara*] must be the first to eat any of it, after which they give permission to their "sisters' sons"... Henceforth they themselves as well as others eat freely of it'. There was a formalized interplay between the rights and obligations of a *bindara* owner and a *mardu* sharer. What is not clear is whether a child's spirit was believed to enter its mother at conception or quickening, or at birth. The Adnjamatana, who were probably influenced by the Dieri, believed that children originated from two mythic women or Mothers, the Maudlangami. On their pendulous breasts were swarms of spirit children (*muri*), whom they told to enter women and so bring about conception. (See Mountford and Harvey 1941: 156.) In this respect they resembled the *julan* (yulan) of the Western Desert, with probably the same relationship between them and the patrilineally-oriented local group (clan, *bindara*). (See Chapter 5.)

Linkages with the Western Aboriginal cultures of the Desert are brought out by Elkin (1934: 173) when he speaks of 'the mythological paths to sacred sites'. The *bindara* was distinguished by its association with a mytho-ritual cycle—and with a piece of territory in relation to which a person's 'totem' and *muramura* had Dreaming significance (Elkin 1931b: 58). *Mura* could be translated as Dreaming. The wanderings of *muramura* creatures were extensive. There were many of them, and some of their myths have been recorded (for example) by Howitt (1904: 475-83, 769-806) and Elkin (1934: 176-92). Among the most important were the *muramura* Gadimargara, a mythical creature of crocodile type, which Elkin (*ibid*.: 176) identifies with a mythic Rainbow Snake (also referred to by Howitt *ibid*.: 801); the *muramura* Margara (yellow-bellied Fish); the *muramura* Birali (Emu's dish), *muramura* Wariliwulu (Bat Man), and *muramura* Darana (Rainmaking Man: see Howitt *ibid*.: 798-800, and Vogelsang 1942); and the *muramura* Mindari (Emu). All such Dreaming creatures left 'tracks', similar to those in the Desert, and sections of these belonged to local *bindara*. Also, each was associated with a number of subsidiary 'totems'. The majority of *muramura* sponsored specific rites which focused on the increase of the natural species—on themselves in 'totemic' form. This aspect of increase was emphasized to a greater extent than in the Western Desert: almost every ritual was performed with this in mind.

As regards initiation, Howitt (*ibid*.: 643-77) includes the Dieri in the 'western tradition'—which, again, brings it relatively close to Desert culture, although there were significant differences at all levels. Circumcision and subincision were involved. One ritual in this sequence was the *maliara* (a word that is used extensively in the Desert as far north as the Walbiri, and also to the north-west: see Meggitt 1966: 3), which refers to the tossing of novices. This meant, symbolically, throwing away 'the old skin that belonged to the novice's childhood'. The *maliara* came into the Dieri country from Macumba, a little to the north-west. After completion of the *wiljaru* (cicatrization) ritual, a youth was given a bullroarer which he had to twirl when out hunting. Once it was handed to him, the young *wiljaru* became 'inspired by the *Mura-mura* of this ceremony, and ... [had] the power to cause a good harvest of snakes and other reptiles by whirling it round ...' (Howitt *ibid*.: 660).

A further non-initiatory ritual was the *mindari* (of the *muramura* Emu). Howitt (*ibid.*: 661-2) and Elkin (*ibid.*: 184-90) have both discussed this. Among other things, it involved inter-moiety cooperation. A large, flattened mud-mound was made and decorated with feathers and ochred dots: this represented the Emu's body. Two women walked across it to the accompaniment of singing; then the mound was broken up, while invocations were called to the Emu to persuade it to breed. In its broken-up state, it looked 'like little emus when they are just born'. An additional rite of 'watering' the decorated emu boomerangs was also intended to increase the supply of emu: the water was brought by women, who later took part in ritual copulation. (See Berndt 1953: 195-6.) The *mindari* was probably one of the most sacred of the Dieri rituals. Executive control was in the hands of men who stood in *bindara* relationship to it; others shared in it on the basis of *mardu* affiliation; and members of other groups (clans) participated too. Women of each moiety were selected to play an active part. Elkin (*ibid.*: 187) says that the *mindari* myth belonged to tribes of south-west Queensland, and extended south to Port Augusta in South Australia. He adds that the Emu myth and its ritual were associated with red-ochre trading, linking economics with religion. It is also highly likely that it was associated with Emu in the Baiami cult of western New South Wales (that is, Emu as wife of Baiami; see below, 3).

Evidence on death is meagre. Gason (1874: 273-5) speaks of restricted cannibalism, when fat from a corpse was removed and eaten: and he notes that fires were placed at the grave-side to warm the deceased. Howitt (*ibid.*: 434) says that the spirit of a deceased person might visit a sleeper: that after death it went into the sky (the Adnjamatana spirit child Mothers also lived in the sky), but would also roam the earth. He says nothing about any specific linkage between a deceased person's spirit on one hand, and spirit children or the *muramura* on the other. However, Elkin (1937: 288-9) speaks of three souls for the Dieri —one of which, the *yada*, goes to a place near Lake Hope and later into the sky. Howitt (*ibid.*: 482) saw a connection between Aranda and Dieri *muramura* beliefs but could find no evidence of reincarnation, such as was common among the Aranda.

Generally, it would seem that the Lake Eyre tribes, and especially the Dieri, represented a type which can be regarded as being culturally intermediate: as having much in common with north-western and western Desert groups, particularly as regards ritual and myth, less as regards social organization: but also heavily influenced by southern Queensland people, and probably too by those in the immediate south, which they influenced perhaps more than they were themselves influenced. Beckett (1967: 456-64) refers to a Maljanga-ba rite of north-western New South Wales, which bears a close resemblance to the Dieri *mura* (*ibid.*: 457) and the *milia* circumcision ceremony (*milia* being a variant of *maliara*). The Desert impact probably came soon after European settlement. That settlement removed the eastern and north-eastern 'cultural cushion' (particularly in north-western New South Wales)—making them, in turn, more vulnerable to consistent interaction with western and north-western Aborigines, who remained culturally intact for a longer period than the Dieri or Lake Eyre people did.

2. THE LOWER RIVER MURRAY

In the southern region, our second example is the lower River Murray people. No-one systematically recorded their traditional culture when it was a living reality. There are early historical sources. More recent research was carried out by Tindale (1937; 1938; 1940) and R. Berndt (mainly unpublished): however, even this material must be classified as 'memory culture'. Today, even that has virtually disappeared.

The Narinyeri constellation comprised several tribes or language units, such as the Yaralde, Tangane, Ramindjeri, Bordaulun, Wargend and lower Gaurna. Each of these was divided into patrilineal territorial totemic clans. In many respects the Narinyeri differed, both socially and culturally, from the peoples to their north. In their social organization, however, there were some superficial resemblances to north-eastern Arnhem Land. Culturally, their links were with the upper Murray and Darling River groups.

The spiritual heritage of a Narinyeri child was reinforced through a name given to it soon after it could walk. This name usually referred to the child's place of birth (Taplin 1873: 51), and to a 'totemic' linkage with a particular territory, either a specific site, or simply clan land. Meyer (1879: 186-7), notes that a child's name was 'frequently derived from some circumstances which occurred at the time of the child's birth'. Each patri-clan had associated with it one or more 'protectors'—it is this association which was conferred on the child. The patri-totem species, in spirit form, was believed to enter the child at birth. What is not clear is the relationship between such 'totems' and the mythic beings.

The major mythic being in this area was Ngurunderi. His myth has been referred to by Taplin (*ibid*.: 55-65), Meyer (*ibid*.: 205-6) and Berndt (1940: 164-85). He was said (by Howitt *ibid*.: 488-9, and by other earlier writers) to be a Supreme Being, responsible for instituting 'all the rites and ceremonies . . . . . practised by the Aborigines, whether connected with life or death'. In the Dreaming, so the myth reports, Ngurunderi travelled down the Murray River in a bark canoe, chasing a large Murray Cod (*pondi*) whose swishing tail formed the river's bends and swamps. Like mythic beings of the Desert and the Dieri, he moved from site to site, naming each one on the basis of a particular incident which occurred there. In the course of his travels he met other mythic beings, such as Nepele, his brother-in-law, the brother of his two wives. At Rawakung, Nepele finally speared the Cod. With the help of Ngurunderi he cut it up, at Pultawar. As they threw each small piece back into the river, they called the name of a fish, and it became that fish. These fish were now 'totemic' protectors. At Ngirlungmurnang, Ngurunderi came upon a group of people whom he transformed into a species of blue bird: this too became a 'totem'. At Larlangangel, he smelled food being cooked by this two wives, who were running away from him. These two, who appear in the Eaglehawk and Crow myth (see Tindale 1941: 259), were originally married to Tulu, Kingfisher, who was killed by Crow: they themselves managed to escape. Ngurunderi also met Parampari, a malignant spirit, and proved invulnerable to his spear thrusts. Eventually he overcame Parampari, and burned him. In his travels, Ngurunderi made many topographical features. But all the time, he was following his wives. Toward the end of the myth, when his wives tried to cross from the mainland to Kangaroo Island, he caused them to drown: they were metamorphosed as rocks, known today as The Pages. Finally, Ngurunderi himself crossed over to Kangaroo Island, named Ngurungaui, and on the western side he cleansed himself in the sea before going into the sky (*waieruwar*), the spirit world.

Several other quite important characters have been reported for this area: Prupe and Koromarange (Tindale 1938), Waiungari (Tindale 1940) and Tjirbuki (Tindale and Mountford 1940). Others again are mentioned by Taplin (*ibid.*: 59-61) and Meyer (*ibid.*: 201-6).

These mythic beings were not themselves 'totemic' or shape-changing: but they con-
formed in other respects with the general picture of Aboriginal mythic characters. They
wandered across the country and down the rivers, changed the shape of the land, and
created or 'turned things into' natural species which could be called 'totemic' as a result
of their association with these sacred beings. However, although Ngurunderi appears to be
of major importance, it would be difficult to grade him in relation to other mythic beings.
All of them were responsible in different ways for establishing the culture of the Narinyeri
people, and all were religious beings. In other words, it does not seem appropriate to speak
of any of them as supreme beings: but they are certainly more prominent than the totem-
protectors tied to specific patri-clans. The Narinyeri themselves, through their totemic
affiliations, were linked indirectly to the great mythic beings. The major difference between
Ngurunderi and the mythic beings of the Narinyeri's northern neighbours is to be found in
that indirect association. Additionally, there is the emphasis on the sky as the Home of
the Dead: Ngurunderi went to this, and (as we shall see) the spirits of the dead were
believed to go there to join him.

Initiation rites for youths (called *narumba*, a word equivalent to sacred or tabu) centred
mainly on food tabus and on depilation of facial hair. A period of rigid segregation was
imposed on novices, to prevent any contact with the non-initiated. They were regarded as
sacred persons, and anything they touched was correspondingly sacred. They even used
reed straws to suck up drinking water, to avoid affecting the general supply. Their state of
sacredness could harm (be too strong or dangerous for) others. Much attention was paid to
instruction. However, there appears to have been no mythic substantiation for the initiatory sequence, as was customary in other regions.

A key to religious life among these lower River Murray people probably lies in the
concept of *narumba*, which Meyer (*ibid.*: 187) calls *rambe* and translates as 'holy'. It
revolved round a complex system of tabus, mostly concerned with food, and some interest-
ing parallels could be drawn with the *kulama* rites of Bathurst and Melville Islands. (See
Part 4.) Complementary to this was an emphasis on increase of natural species, not
necessarily entailing collective rites in the accepted Aboriginal fashion. Material on ritual
events among the Narinyeri is very sparse. Meyer (*ibid.*: 203) mentions large meetings,
when 'dancing and singing men represented their ancestors'. Taplin (*ibid.*: 37) speaks of the
ringbalin, at which men danced and women sang. He also says that some *ringbalin* were
used 'as a charm to frighten away disease'—which, again, draws it close to the Bathurst and
Melville Islands *kulama*. In unpublished material (recorded by R. Berndt), sacred rituals
attended by men and women included dancing that dramatized the behaviour of various
natural species, the clan totems. Many of these dances were of increase intent. Power to
increase these species rested in the mythic beings initially responsible for their coming into
being. Taplin (*ibid.*: 55) refers to a ceremony that took place during a hunting trip—a
wallaby was burnt, to the accompaniment of upraised spears and invocations. He remarks
that this was instituted by Ngurunderi.

Death, however, was mythologically substantiated by Matamai, the son of Ngurunderi
and sometimes identified with him. It was he who dessicated the first human body, and
this became a traditional practice among the lower River Murray people (see Taplin

ibid.: 18-22; Meyer *ibid.*: 187-200). Ngurunderi, before he cleansed himself and went into the sky (the spirit-world), told the Yaralde that spirits of the dead would always follow the tracks he had made to Kangaroo Island: they 'would go up to Waieruwar and reside with him' (Berndt 1940: 182). Taplin (*ibid.*: 18-19, 141-2) said that all these people expected to go to Waieruwar after death: he added that the dead were believed to come down from the sky and injure those whom they disliked. Also, it was said that people were believed to live on after death, that the spirit was like a shadow, and that spirits of the dead were feared. The cycle is incomplete because, although human spirits return to Ngurunderi, the sky world is also the abode of the mythic beings—virtually all of them are represented in various stars and constellations: and re-birth was not specifically underlined, since it was achieved through the intermediate 'protectors' or 'totems' of the local clans.

3. South-Eastern Australia

The spread of culture along the main waterways such as the Murray and the Darling provides a clue to religious differences and similarities. The Narinyeri, distinctive as they were, had much in common with groups in northern Victoria and south-western New South Wales. Howitt (*ibid.*: 488-508) noted that south-east Australia was unusual in its All-Father belief: this is the Supreme Being concept that Taplin took up. Howitt provides an assortment of evidence beginning with Ngurunderi, and including Baiamban (or Baiami), Nurelli (the Narinyeri Nepele), Bunyil, Daramulun and Munganngaua, among others. All of these mythic beings eventually went into the sky. Some were closely linked with others and all, presumably, had special myths associated with them. Many were spoken of as 'father', and were conceived of as being in human form even when they had names of natural species attached to them. Most had creative qualities. Rituals, usually initiatory, were held in their honour or were stimulated by them: and they were said to be present at these. In one such rite (Woeworung; Howitt *ibid.*: 492), an incident in the life of Bunyil was enacted and 'images .. carved in bark were exhibited'. Among the Yuin (*ibid.*: 494-5), Daramulun made the first *kuringal* or *bora* initiation rites and introduced the bullroarer, which when swung was the sound of his voice.

Baiami was especially significant to the Wuradjeri, according to material collected in recent years (R. Berndt 1947: 327-65, 60-86) as well as from earlier sources (for example, Howitt, *ibid.*; Curr 1886-7; Ridley 1875; Smyth 1878; also see Elkin 1963). Among them, totem-inheritance was matrilineal: and magic was integrated with religion. For instance, myths about Wild Turkey and Eaglehawk, Crow and Robin Red Breast, and Red Kangaroo substantiated various forms of magic and at the same time sponsored the initiation of native doctors (see also Elkin 1945). Further, much of what is now labelled as magic was, in the past, part of sacred ritual. 'Clever men', it was said, could commune with Baiami. A child would commence his training as a 'clever man' even before his ordinary initiation. The child's spirit (*warangun*) would be taken by a 'clever man' on his nocturnal wanderings, or when he went into the sky to obtain rain. Howitt mentions a man who had been taken by his father to the 'camp of Baiami' beyond the sky and gave a description of Daramulun.

Also of importance was the *jarawaiewa* (yarawaiyewa), a patrilineal assistant totem which differed from the *djindji* (the totem derived from the mother): the *djindji* was called 'meat' or 'flesh', referring to emu flesh sacred to Baiami. (For reference to the social organization, see Elkin 1933: 112-3, 136-7.) During the process of initiation, a father would take his son away to a secret place and sing into him the spirit-double of his own assistant totem (the *jarawaiewa*.) In this way, that totem spirit merged with the youth's own spirit (his *warangun*). Baiami also presided at the making of 'clever men' and is said to have brought forth from his mouth sacred water, *kali*, liquefied quartz crystal possessing great magical power. After tooth-evulsion, at initiation, sacred rites were held at a *bulpa* cere-monial ring linked by a *tarampol* pathway to a *wilkandja* or sacred 'play ground'. Women assembled at the *bulpa*, and waited, covered up, while the *taramulin* (Daramulun) bullroarer was swung; its 'voice' was the voice of Baiami. Then they sang and danced, while men performed magical feats. Nests related to the Eaglehawk myth were constructed in trees on the *wilkandja*, and one of the concluding rites was an exchange of wives for coitus. Emu meat was tabu to all youths and men who had not undergone the special rite associated with it: the normalizing rite took place some time after ordinary initiation. Emu was 'the food of Baiami', but was also the wife of Daramulun (often an alternative name for Baiami). She was also called Kurikuta, and was the mother of Crow. Some myth-versions claim that the emu was her assistant totem, but usually they were identified together. Apart from the tabu on eating emu meat and the rite to terminate that prohibition, the cooking of an emu was said to disturb Kurikuta. Should the fat of a roasting emu burn as a result of careless cooking, the resulting smoke would almost certainly attract Kurikuta: she would descend from the sky, revealing her quartz crystal body in a brilliant flash of lightning with a great burst of thunder. This belief was widespread, and was noted by Mathews (1904: 345) and others. It is probable that the *mindari* of the Dieri was linked, as already noted, with the emu rituals of western New South Wales.

In Wuradjeri belief, all 'totemic' beings went to a place named Wantanggangura, 'beyond the clouds and sky'. There were many such beings in the mythology. A description of this Sky Land is given by Berndt (*ibid.*: 361-5).

Howitt (*ibid.*: 583-88) and Mathews (1897a) have discussed the *burbung* initiation rituals of the Wiradjeri (Wuradjeri) and associated tribes. The *burbung* (probably the *bulpa*) closely resembled the *kuringal*. Rites were marked off in a series of stages by particular representations: for instance, a spiral piece of bark signified the path between the sky and the earth. On the ground a figure of Daramulun was cut (as son of Baiami, not Baiami himself as among the Yuin), with his axe, emu tracks, and the emu itself. At each stage, magic-dances were held, presided over by 'clever men'.

The *bora* rituals of New South Wales were, as far as we know, primarily initiatory. Howitt (*ibid.*: 509-642), among others, provides a wide coverage of these, which he classifies as belonging to the eastern type, in contrast to the Dieri and Western Desert variety. He places the Narinyeri rites in the latter category. (It will be recalled that in Section 2 of this Chapter they are seen as being quite separate, but influenced by the eastern type.)

The *kuringal* of the Yuin was marked by a circular ring of earth, within which the pre-liminary rites took place: this was connected by a path to a sacred enclosure, just as in the case of the *bulpa* and *wilkandja* (see above). Along the pathway, men were shown various representations, emblems or figures, each associated with native doctors ('clever men'). Howitt (*ibid.*: 522-4) mentions a grave at which a 'clever man' danced, exhibiting quartz crystal between his teeth. Other items were an ant-eater made of earth, a clay figure of a brown snake, and a life-size figure of Daramulun made out of earth, surrounded by weapons and implements. Invocations were called to Baiami (whose secret name in this context was said to be Daramulun), and bullroarers were swung. After a long initiation period designed to make novices acceptable to Daramulun, a stretch of ground was prepared, and holes were dug for the novices to stand in. Then a life-size figure of Daramulun was cut in relief upon a stringybark tree: and in front of this, and the novices, men danced in bark-fibre disguises while a mound was beaten with a strip of bark. The novices had their upper incisor teeth removed and were led to the Daramulun tree, where they were told of his powers, that he lived behind the sky, and that, when a man died Daramulun would take care of him (*ibid.*: 543). Subsequent rituals, according to Howitt, were held to illustrate the magical powers of the clever men. Additionally, there was a range of 'totemic' perform-ances, one including the dances of Daramulun and Ngalalbal (Emu). As far as the 'totemic' dances are concerned, it seems likely that these refer to the matrilineal totems—but this is uncertain; some could relate to assistant totems which were themselves connected with magic. Virtually all the performances referred to by Howitt are actually of magical signif-icance, or designed to demonstrate the power of clever men. Further rites consisted of making a figure of Daramulun with an elongated penis, and dancing around it. Also, there was a wide range of food restrictions, especially on emu meat.

Without providing further descriptions, it will be obvious that these initiation sequences differ considerably from those that are discussed in Chapters 4 and 5. The main point of difference is not so much the isolated rite of tooth-evulsion, which is widespread throughout Aboriginal Australia in one form or another, but the structure of the initiation ground with its pathway linking the earth (*bulpa*) with the sky (symbolized by the sacred *wilkan-dja*). The contrast is enhanced by the use of earth- and clay-moulded representations of mythic beings (especially Baiami/Daramulun), the performance of magic dances and actions, and the special participation of clever men. However, a reassessment of existing material is needed. Much that has been classified as 'magical' by a number of writers (including Berndt 1947) could equally well be described as sacred. Further, the assistant totems, previously considered to be associated only with clever men, can be regarded as an integral part of religious ritual. Although 'totemic' dances were held, this was usually in a 'magical' context, and they were subsidiary to rites centring on the major being Daramulun or Baiami. The relationship of these 'totemic' creatures to Baiami is not clearly defined. They were certainly associated with him in some way, as their myths and ritual reenactments indicate, and some were concerned with food restrictions. Of these, the emu was the most outstanding. It was not without reason that some of the earlier writers saw Baiami as a dominant being, and a Sky God at that.

One possible explanation here is that the religious ideology of this region expressed man's preoccupation with a Hereafter. In saying that, it would be necessary to admit that the rest of Aboriginal Australia is interested in the Hereafter as, in effect, the Here and Now. In the *kuringal*, *burbung* and *bora*, the 'totemic' dances do not seem to be, at least not directly, associated with fertility, not in the same sense as elsewhere.

In the rites surrounding spirits of the dead and death itself, similar themes appear. Following a death, the malignant aspect of the *warangun* became a *djir*. The *djirguti* rite (Berndt *ibid.*: 344-50) took place on a cleared ground, and women beat drum pads. Dancing men would posture with two cut-bark figures of *djir*: quartz crystals were said to be magic-ally projected from the *djir* effigies into the dancing men, and later removed by clever men.

After death the *warangun* was gradually obliterated by the *djir* (or *jir* of Howitt *ibid.*: 439, 465-6), and it was the assistant totem which travelled to the sky world to join the immortals.

Two further implications can be noted, in contrasting this south-eastern religious complex with others. The Lévi-Straussian opposition of matrilineal and patrilineal elements is well expressed in the physical attributes of the *warangun-djir*, and the spiritual attribute of the assistant totem which links a person to magico-religious ritual on one hand and ensures his entry to the Sky World on the other.

One problem here is the *djindji*, the matrilineal totem, and the degree to which it is identified with the *warangun*. From the evidence, it seems that the two must be envisaged as separate. If assistant totems were so important in ritual, what of the ritual importance of the *djindji*, especially as it was significant in relation to emu meat and especially too because of the emu's association with Baiami's wife? The totems relevant to matrilineal totemic clans, themselves distributed between the matrilineal moieties, along with a large number of natural species represented in the religious mythology, were all connected with Baiami.

The other problem is an especially difficult one because the evidence is incomplete. Human beings made ritual contacts with the mythic characters whom they regarded as creators and as instigators of ritual. But they were not apparently identified with man: man was not, as far as we know, regarded as a manifestation of his mythic beings. Apparently, too, a person saw himself as being distinct from his assistant totem, as being in control of it but not one with it. And it was this which escaped to the Sky World on death, leaving behind it the *warangun-djir*—the 'earth-bound' personality of man.

THE ICONOGRAPHIC CONTEXT

This south-eastern region is particularly uneven as regards information on material representations. For the lower River Murray (Narinyeri), few ritual objects have survived. As far as we know, there were no carvings or paintings of Ngurunderi or associated mythic beings. Worsnop (1897: 148) mentioned the use of a bullroarer in initiation. In the so-called 'totemic' rituals of probable increase intent or in dancing relating to the clan ancestors, the Narinyeri seem the have relied on body painting and on head decorations. Along with the concept of *narumba*, the dessicated bodies of the dead probably epitomized sacredness (in a tangible way) without the necessity of any further outward sign.

The Lake Eyre Basin cultures, represented primarily by the Dieri, were remarkable for their *muramura* rituals. These paralleled closely the separate mythic sequences of the Western Desert. Although a great deal of this material is still in manuscript form (as it is for the Narinyeri), each *muramura* had associated with it a particular ritual patterning and particular emblemic headdresses, etc. (See Horne and Aiston 1924: figs. 78, 79.) Stirling and Waite (1919: 105-55, Plates XI-XX) discuss the *muramura*, who were regarded as creative beings, and who left (were metamorphosed as, 'turned into') stones which were smeared with red-ochre. Vogelsang (1942) provides one example of these stones. They represented powerful relics of a secret-sacred nature, and were central to cult activity. In addition to these were the *toas*, signposts or indicators of particular *muramura* localities. Each *toa*, by its shape, colour, design or appendages, depicted certain conspicuous or outstanding topographic features, or referred to episodes in the wanderings of *muramura*. These were not used ritually, but indicated the place to which a particular person or group had gone. A significant point here is that interpreting any *toa* sign called for considerable knowledge of a wide range of local *muramura* mythology. In one sense, these were comparable to the secret-sacred *tjurunga* designs. However, in the Dieri case they were not necessarily of *tjurunga* shape, although some of them were.

The Dieri *mindari* was essentially of *muramura* type, although it was apparently of more general social importance and was not restricted to its own local group. In the *mindari*, the flattened mud-mound with its red-ochre and feathers representing the Emu *muramura* brings to mind the ritually decorated mounds and ground paintings of Central Australia. The bullroarer was also a feature of Dieri initiation, after cicatrization had taken place.

In south-eastern Australia, in New South Wales and northern Victoria, initiation included magico-religious ritual: bullroarers were used; and, iconographically, the shape of dancing and ritual grounds was significant. There was the presence of images, in human and in non-human form. Life-size figures of Daramulun were exhibited in bark, cut into a tree, or modelled in clay or built up on the ground. Thomas (1906: Plate 28) provided an early illustration from Port Stephens, in which a figure of Daramulun is represented by a pole with a long conical cap, and a crosspiece as arms. There were models of animals, tools, weapons, and so on. These can probably be compared with the 'totemic' creatures, realistically made, in the western Arnhem Land *maraiin*, and at Aurukun in Queensland (McCarthy 1964).

BIBLIOGRAPHY

Beckett, J. 1967. Marriage, Circumcision and Avoidance among the Maljangaba of North-west N.S.W., *Mankind*, Vol. 6, No. 10.
Berndt, R. M. 1940. Some Aspects of Jaralde Culture, South Australia, *Oceania*, Vol. XI, No. 2.
Berndt, R. M. 1947. Wuradjeri Magic and 'Clever Men', *Oceania*, Vol. XVII, No. 4; Vol. XVIII, No. 1.
Berndt, R. M. 1953. A Day in the Life of a Dieri Man before Alien Contact, *Anthropos*, Vol. 48.
Berndt, R. M. 1963. Groups with Minimal European Associations. In *Australian Aboriginal Studies* (H. Sheils, ed.).
Corris, P. 1968. *Aborigines and Europeans in Western Victoria*: Ethnohistory Series No. 1, Occasional Papers in Aboriginal Studies No. 12, Australian Institute of Aboriginal Studies, Canberra.
Curr, E. M. 1886-87. *The Australian Race*: Government Printer, Melbourne (Trübner, London), 4 vols.
Elkin, A. P. 1931a. The Kopara. The Settlement of Grievances, *Oceania*, Vol. II, No. 2.
Elkin, A. P. 1931b. The Social Organization of South Australian Tribes, *Oceania*, Vol. II, No. 1.
Elkin, A. P. 1933. *Studies in Australian Totemism*: Oceania Monographs, No. 2, Australian National Research Council, Sydney.
Elkin, A. P. 1934. Cult-Totemism and Mythology in Northern South Australia, *Oceania*, Vol. V, No. 2.
Elkin, A. P. 1937. Beliefs and Practices connected with Death in north-eastern and western South Australia, *Oceania*, Vol. VII, No. 3.
Elkin, A. P. 1945. *Aboriginal Men of High Degree*: Australasian Publishing Co., Sydney.
Elkin, A. P. 1963. The Development of Scientific Knowledge of the Aborigines. In *Australian Aboriginal Studies* (H. Sheils, ed.).
Fison, L. and A. W. Howitt. 1880. *Kamilaroi and Kurnai*: G. Robertson, Melbourne.
Fry, H. K. 1937. Dieri Legends, *Folklore*, Vol. 48.
Gason, S. 1874. *The Manners and Customs of the Dieyerie Tribe of Australian Aborigines*: Adelaide. Also in *The Native Tribes of South Australia* (J. D. Woods, ed.), 1879.
Horne, G. and G. Aiston. 1924. *Savage Life in Central Australia*: Macmillan, London.
Howitt, A. W. 1904. *The Native Tribes of South-East Australia*: Macmillan, London.
Lévi-Strauss, C. 1963. *Totemism*: Beacon Press, Boston. (R. Needham, trans.).
Mathew, J. 1899. *Eaglehawk and Crow. A Study of the Australian Aborigines*: Nutt, London.

Mathews, R. H. 1897a. The Burbung, or Initiation Ceremonies of the Murrumbidgee Tribes, *Journal and Proceedings of the Royal Society of New South Wales*, Vol. XXI.

Mathews, R. H. 1897b. The Totemic Divisions of Australian Tribes, *Journal of the Royal Society of New South Wales*, Vol. XXXI.

Mathews, R. H. 1904. Ethnological Notes on the Aboriginal Tribes of New South Wales and Victoria, *Journal and Proceedings of the Royal Society of New South Wales*, Vol. XXXVIII.

McCarthy, F. D. 1964. The Dancers of Aurukun, *Australian Natural History*, Vol. 14, No. 9.

Meggitt, M. J. 1966. *Gadjari among the Walbiri Aborigines of Central Australia*: Oceania Monographs, No. 14, University of Sydney, Sydney.

Meyer, H.E.A. 1879. *Manners and Customs of the Aborigines of the Encounter Bay Tribe, South Australia*: Adelaide; originally published in 1846. In *The Native Tribes of South Australia* (J. D. Woods, ed.).

Mountford, C. P. and A. Harvey. 1941. Women of the Adnjamatana Tribe of the Northern Flinders Ranges, South Australia, *Oceania*, Vol. XII, No. 2.

Parker, K. L. 1905. *The Euahlayi Tribe*: Constable, London.

Ridley, W. 1875. *Kamilaroi and other Australian Languages*: T. Richards, Government Printer, Sydney.

Sheils, H. ed. 1963. *Australian Aboriginal Studies*: Oxford University Press, Melbourne.

Siebert, O. 1910. Sagen und Sitten der Dieri, *Globus*, Vol. 97, Nos. 3-4.

Smith, J. 1880. *The Booandik Tribe of South Australian Aborigines* ...: Government Printer, Adelaide.

Smyth, R. Brough. 1878. *The Aborigines of Victoria* ...: Government Printer, Melbourne, 2 vols.

Stirling, E. and E. R. Waite. 1919. Description of Toas, or Australian Aboriginal Direction Signs, *Records of the South Australian Museum*, Vol. I, No. 2.

Taplin, G. 1873. *The Narrinyeri*: Adelaide. Also in *The Native Tribes of South Australia* (J. D. Woods, ed.).

Taplin, G. 1879. *The Folklore, manners, customs, and languages of the South Australian Aborigines*: Government Printer, Adelaide.

Thomas, N. W. 1906. *Natives of Australia*: Constable, London.

Tindale, N. B. 1937. Native Songs of the South-East of South Australia, *Transactions of the Royal Society of South Australia*, Vol. 61.

Tindale, N. B. 1938. Prupe and Koromarange, a Legend of the Tanganekald, Coorong, South Australia, *Transactions of the Royal Society of South Australia*, Vol. 61.

Tindale, N B. 1940. Legend of Waijungari, Jaralde Tribe, Lake Alexandrina, South Australia ... *Records of the South Australian Museum*. Vol. V, No. 3.

Tindale, N. B. 1941. Eagle and Crow myths of the Maraura Tribe, Lower Darling River, New South Wales, *Records of the South Australian Museum*, Vol. VI, No. 3.

Tindale, N. B. and C. P. Mountford. 1940. Results of the Excavation of Kongarati Cave near Second Valley, South Australia, *Records of the South Australian Museum*, Vol. V, No. 4.

Vogelsang, T. 1942. Hearts of the Two Sons of the Mura Mura Darana—Ceremonial Objects of the Dieri Tribe, South Australia, *Records of the South Australian Museum*, Vol. VII, No. 2.

Woods, J. D. ed. 1879. *The Native Tribes of South Australia*: Wigg, Adelaide.

Worsnop, T. 1897. *The Prehistoric Arts, Manufactures, Works, Weapons, etc., of the Aborigines of Australia*: Government Printer, Adelaide.

ILLUSTRATIONS

PREAMBLE

Since this Fascicle includes Chapter One, as a general view of Australian Aboriginal religion, the illustrations provided here are drawn from several different areas, which will be considered in other Fascicles. Although selection of these has rested on iconographic considerations, I have purposely avoided a museum-style presentation except for a very few, preferring to set such material objects wherever possible in their social context. Some cave paintings appear in this Fascicle, and a small range of bark paintings. But mostly, as throughout these Fascicles, the iconography is seen in its relationship to the people themselves, and as part of their religious experience.

Relevant to Chapter Two of this Fascicle, some old photographs are reproduced. The series on the south-eastern Australian *bora* rituals contain the only photographs which have survived of the earth figures of Baiami-Daramulun variety and of linear designs cut in sand. The ceremonial life of the lower River Murray in South Australia is represented by two old drawings. Lake Eyre Basin material, of Dieri-type, is just as rare: very little 'live' ritual material has survived, although large collections of religious items were made.

ACKNOWLEDGEMENTS

I gratefully acknowledge the help of the following persons who have made available photographic material. Mr. Eric Brandl of the Welfare Division of the Northern Territory Administration, has supplied figures 27 to 32. Figures 42 to 55 of the *bora* rituals have been provided by Tyrrell and Co. Ltd. of Sydney. Originally, these were old glass plates taken by Kerry and have been reproduced in other studies. The two lower River Murray drawings (Figures 40 and 41) are reproduced from *South Australia Illustrated* by George French Angas, London, 1847, Plate XV, and were photographed originally by the Public Library of South Australia (1943). The Dieri-type photographs were kindly provided by Mr. Robert Edwards, Curator of Anthropology of the South Australian Museum. These, Figures 33 to 39, came from the George Aiston collection. Figures 15 to 20 were generously supplied by Mr. Roy Thorne of the Elcho Island mission settlement, Arnhem Land. All the others were taken by the author himself on the field, or are photographs of objects collected by him.

Some of the figures illustrated here have also been published previously in various works. There is no point in detailing all of these, although the following comments provide some indication and refer to books and not to articles.

Figures 8 to 14 also appear in *Art in Arnhem Land* by A. P. Elkin, R. M. and C. H. Berndt, Melbourne, 1950, although not necessarily in their present form. Figure 21 is shown in *Australian Aboriginal Art*, edited by R. M. Berndt, Sydney 1964. Figure 23 is illustrated in *Aboriginal Man in Australia*, edited by R. M. and C. H. Berndt, Sydney, 1965.

Figures 33 to 39 should be compared with those in G. Horne and G. Aiston, *Savage Life in Central Australia*, London, 1924: our Figure 39 is the same as one published there, but the others are not although there are certain similarities. Figures 40 and 41 appeared originally in G. F. Angas's volume (*op. cit.*). Figures 42 to 56 have been illustrated in various publications over the years: for instance, Figure 45 is in F. D. McCarthy, *Australian Aboriginal Decorative Art*, Australian Museum, Sydney, 1958; and Figures 42, 43, 46 and 56 are in A. Massola, *The Aborigines of south-eastern Australia. As they were*, Melbourne, 1971, but—as far as I know—all that I produce here have not been assembled together.

Description of Figures

Figure 1. Painting a *djuwei* post for use in the *djunggawon* circumcisional ritual at Elcho Island in north-eastern Arnhem Land, within the 'Murngin' cultural area. See Fascicle Two, Chapter Four, *ii*. The photograph was taken in 1961 by R. Berndt. The post is a conventionalized representation of the elder Wawalag sister, a mythic being who with her younger sister was swallowed by the Yulunggul Python: they sponsor the great *dua* moiety Wawalag cycle of rituals. The post itself is her body and the bound stringy bark is her hair. The artist, using a human-hair brush, is painting a design of red *ridjangu* berries which she collected in her travels. Beside him are a palette on which he mixes his ochres, and grinding stones used in preparing them. Artist: Galbagalba, of the Djambarbingu dialect group. See also Figures 2 and 7.

Figure 2. As in Figure 1. Two *djuwei* being prepared for the *djunggawon* ritual. On the left is the post representing the elder Wawalag sister (shown in Figure 1); on the right, the younger sister—artist, Wolaliba, Galbu dialect unit. Elcho Island, 1961: collected by R. Berndt.

Figure 3. A men's camp at Elcho Island, 1961: ritual objects are being made and men are painting on sheets of stringy bark. In the foreground is an upright *wuramu* figure used in *jiridja* moiety mortuary rituals. See Fascicle Two, Chapter Four, *iii*. Such a figure is a memorial to the deceased person, a visible representation of his spiritual secret-sacred linkage with the Dreaming. It is also a focus of the *mogwoi* aspect of his spirit which remains on the home ground while its other aspect, the *birimbir*, goes to the Island of the Dead. The designs in this case are associated with the Waramiri dialect unit: the triangles are clouds, derived from the spray of a mythic *wimari* whale: the object itself is similar to a secret-sacred *rangga* emblem. The artists are Njambi and Mambur (for Ngulberei), Waramiri dialect unit. From R. Berndt.

Figure 4. Dancing in a *jiridja* moiety mortuary ritual at Yirrkalla, in north-eastern Arnhem Land, 1964. See Fascicle Two, Chapter Four, *iii*. The flags signify farewell to the deceased's spirit who goes to the *jiridja* moiety Island of the Dead. From R. Berndt.

Figure 5. A *wuramu* mortuary figure at Elcho Island which, after the relevant rituals, is left to rot. It represents a deceased *jiridja* moiety man and serves as a memorial. In the background are Aboriginal camps. Made originally by Wulainbuma, Waramiri dialect unit. R. Berndt, 1968.

Figure 6. Sacred emblemic patterning of the Riradjingu dialect unit painted on the side of a modern canoe and used in a dedication rite to ensure its protection and also aid in fishing. Yirrkalla, 1968.

On the left-hand side is a painting of two turtles swimming; the surrounding lines are waves. These are associated with the *dua* moiety mythic being Mururuma, the Bremer Island (close to Yirrkalla settlement) Turtle man, a famous turtle hunter and headman. His spirit centre is at the Muruwiri Rocks. The two turtles are also mythic: one the green-backed turtle man, Marban, the other his wife, Woiaba; both are now rocks.

The right-hand painting is of Bodngu the Thunder man at Yilgaba Hill (Mt. Dundas), near Yirrkalla and Gove; he urinates rain. He holds long yams (which appear to hang from his elbows, but he is actually holding their creeper-strings), which symbolize the thunder bolts he throws to the ground. The lines surrounding him are clouds and beach. The three dark circles (at the bottom left) are round rocks, *mililg*, his 'eyes'.

These patterns are similar to those painted on bark, and traditionally used in sacred ritual.

Figure 7. This *djuwei* post is the same as depicted in Figure 1. In this case, its trunk-painting has been completed. The elder Wawalag sister has had her hair of shredded bark arranged, and on it a feathered string with pendants as a chaplet. On her head (above the string) is a design representing small stones over which the Two Sisters walked while in Wagilag country, to the south, on their way to the sacred waters of Muruwul where Yulunggul was living. Below her 'hair' is a design of red *ridjangu* berries and, below that again, leaves of the berry bush. Collected by R. Berndt, 1961: now in the Department of Anthropology, University of Western Australia: height, 2.50 feet.

Figure 8. The younger Wawalag sister. See Figure 2, also Figure 7. Her breasts are those of a young girl, and the ridge between them is a cicatrization scar. She wears a feathered string chaplet with hanging tassels on her head, and a *maidga* string breast-girdle, and a pubic apron. Her facial designs represent a headband; on her cheeks, the stains from rain made by the Yulunggul Python; and under her chin, eucalypt flowers (*durilji*) associated with her in song cycles. On her body are further rain marks, a boomerang pattern (from the far south, since boomerangs are not normally used in north-eastern Arnhem Land), and below these menstrual blood, a major emphasis in the cycle. At her thighs (which can just be seen) are cuts, signifying the circumcision of her husband. This unique example was carved and painted by Mawulan, of the Riradjingu dialect unit: it is 32 inches in height. It was obtained by R. Berndt at Yirrkalla in 1946-47, and is now housed in the Institute of Anatomy collection, Canberra.

Figure 9. This is Laindjung, the great mythic being of the *jiridja* moiety. See Fascicle Three, Chapter Four continued, under Fertility Rites. Laindjung or Banaidja emerged from the sea at Blue Mud Bay, south of Yirrkalla in north-eastern Arnhem Land. His face is stained white from the sea foam, and on his body are the variegated water-marks which formed patterns and became the sacred emblemic designs of *jiridja* dialect units. On the flattened top of his head, human hair has been fastened with blood. At each corner of his mouth are parrakeet feathers, his moustache. A feathered chin-pendant is his beard. His head has a painted band used only for ritual dancing; and the band from ear to ear, passing across the nose, is a special decoration used only in his ritual. On his left arm is a feathered armband. The decorations on the upper part of his body refer to his sacred mythology: a design of fire or ashes inside seaweed and mud, referring to the Dalwongu and Mararba dialect units. Around his neck is a fresh-water weed design, of the Dalwongu dialect unit. Laindjung in his Banaidja form is a barramundi fish; in the secret-sacred *jiridja* moiety *nara* rituals a paperbark pad is beaten, and the sound is his voice. The full height of this figure is 36.50 inches. The artists are Liagarang, Dalwongu dialect unit and Munggaraui, Gumaidj dialect unit. Obtained at Yirrkalla by R. Berndt in 1946-47 and now in the Institute of Anatomy collection, Canberra.

Figure 10. Kultana who, with her husband, is a mythic being associated with the *jiridja* moiety Land of the Dead. They belong to the Gumaidj dialect unit, but live on the mythical island of Modilnga, north of the Wessell Islands: there they light grass fires to attract spirits of the dead. In this illustration, Kultana has shoulder-length hair made of shredded bark. The vertical bands painted on her face and body are rain streaming down; she is also responsible for sending the cold *jiridja* winds.

This figure (full height, 36.50 inches) was made by Munggaraui, of the Gumaidj dialect unit. It was obtained at Yirrkalla by R. Berndt in 1946-47 and is now in the Department of Anthropology, University of Western Australia.

Figure 11. This bark painting in local ochres depicts a mortuary scene. The central figure is an exposed corpse lying on a platform raised on four forked sticks: it is painted with the dead person's sacred mythic pattern: at each side, close to the body, darkened elongated ovals are small paperbark effigies painted in ochres, symbolizing the deceased's children. On the right-hand side, is the person responsible for the man's death: he is shown in his spirit form spearing him. On the left-hand side is the decomposed corpse some time afterward, ready for bone collection. Surrounding it are maggots. At the left centre, bones are being collected and placed in a bark coffin, also painted with the dead man's dialect unit emblems. The rest of the surrounding panel is made up of dancing men (below) 'helping the deceased's spirit', sending it to the Island of the Dead; right, women dancing and wailing while they gash their heads in mourning; top, a woman wailing, a didjeridu player, and a songman with clapping sticks. See Fascicle Two, Chapter Four, *iii*.

The artist is Yama a Gumaidj dialect unit man. The painting was obtained at Yirrkalla in 1946-47 by R. Berndt and is now in the Department of Anthropology, University of Western Australia.

Figure 12. This is a Gumaidj dialect unit sacred pattern connected with Daliwi (or Dalywoi Bay) near Cape Arnhem in north-eastern Arnhem Land. The top left-hand panel shows a large diamond stingray surrounded by 'queen' fish: at each side are black rain clouds with bands of falling rain. The right-hand, top, panel shows further clouds and rain, with a yellow *gulgmin* water snake which is really the penis of Bodngu (see Figure 6), who in this case is responsible for the rain: the *gulgmin* makes lightning by flickering its forked tongue: two 'queen' fish are with it. In the middle band are mangrove stingray: dots are bubbles rising to the surface of the water, and bars with circles are their holes: there is a 'tortoise shell' turtle and more mangrove stingray. Below are stingray and the sacred Gumaidj crocodile floating on the surface of the water, surrounded by fish, and with rain falling on its head: also further rain clouds, rain and fish. When the rain falls, the mangrove stingray go to the river banks to spawn.

The artist is Bununggu, a Gumaidj dialect unit man. The painting was collected in 1946-47 by R. Berndt and is in the collection of the Department of Anthropology, University of Western Australia.

Figure 13. A bark painting of a sacred pattern from the *jiridja* moiety Waramiri dialect unit, north-eastern Arnhem Land. It is associated with Malgura, at Cape Wilberforce. At the top is a row of 'mother' stingrays; the middle bands are a sandbank; in the lower panel is a row of newly born stingray. At birth the 'mother' stingray deposits its young on the opposite side of the sandbank. The criss-cross design surrounding these creatures represents the discolouration of the shallow water caused by their stirring up the mud.

The artists are Mau, a Djabu dialect man and Wondjug, a Riradjingu dialect man; both are of the *dua* moiety but have *jiridja* moiety affiliations through their mothers. Collected in 1946-47 at Yirrkalla by R. Berndt. Now in the collection of the Department of Anthropology, University of Western Australia.

Figure 14. This is a sacred Gumaidj dialect unit pattern. It concerns the mythic crocodile associated with Laindjung-Banaidja (see Figure 9), from Blue Mud Bay in north-eastern Arnhem Land. In the Dreaming, the crocodile made a shelter on a ritual ground in which secret-sacred *rangga* pole emblems (see Fascicle Three) were stored. A fire, however, accidentally destroyed the shelter and the *rangga*, as well as some of the men. The crocodile burned his 'arms' and escaped to Caledon Bay, taking fire with him. The painting depicts country along a saltwater river, from coastal billabong and bush to the beach. On the right is the long-armed crocodile surrounded by seaweed lying on a bed of mud: white dots among the foliage are seaweed flowers and black dots are bubbles rising to the surface of the water as the crocodile moves among the seaweed. On the left is his son, a short-armed crocodile (who burned his 'arms' in the Dreaming fire); around him are seaweed, flowers and bubbles; two bream fish are his food.

The artist is Munggaraui, Gumaidj dialect unit, and the painting was collected at Yirrkalla in 1946-47 by R. Berndt. It is now in the Department of Anthropology, University of Western Australia.

Figures 15 to 20 cover scenes from a delayed-mortuary ritual series held at Yirrkalla in September 1968, for Mawulan, a Riradjingu headman who died in November 1967. The complete series is complex and colourful, and both *dua* and *jiridja* moiety people participate; some aspects of it are of an especially sacred character. It is held on the main dancing ground above the beach at Yirrkalla and the line of movement is toward the area where the interment took place. A further selection from this same mortuary series is illustrated in Fascicle Two, Figures 44 to 49.

Figure 15. This illustration shows a typical male dancer daubed with white pipe clay: he is Mawulan's son. Wondjug. Around his neck is a fighting bag, which is used in dancing; in fighting, a man holds it between his teeth. He carries a spearthrower decorated with a wild honey design (associated with the mythic being Woial, who has links with the Wawalag sisters). In the background are decorated participants, men and women.

Photo: R. Thorne, Yirrkalla, 1968.

Figure 16. This figure depicts ritual goanna posturing of the *dua* moiety, associated with the great Djanggawul mytho-ritual cycle. (See Fascicle Three, Chapter Four continued, under Fertility Rites.) The central actor has parrakeet-feathered armlets with tassels tipped with sea-gull feathers. On the right are a man playing a didjeridu, and a songman with clapping-sticks. The ritual action, carried out in the open camp, represents an extremely sacred section of the Djanggawul myth.

Photo: R. Thorne, Yirrkalla, 1968.

Figure 17. Upright *rangga* emblems of 'outside' (non-secret) variety, decorated in ochre designs, refer to the Wawalag mythology (see Figures 1, 2, 7, and 8), to the mythic being Woial, and to honey bees. The central figure is brushing a participant with eucalypt leaves: this neutralizes the powerful supernatural influences that are inseparable from such rites, and especially from viewing sacred objects, which contain the spiritual substance of the mythic beings themselves.

Photo: R. Thorne, Yirrkalla, 1968.

Figure 18. This figure is within the same sequence. Here, men dance part of the cycle focused on Bralgu, the *dua* moiety Land of the Dead. They represent *mogwoi* spirits—not the deceased's earth-bound *mogwoi* spirit but Dreaming *mogwoi* at Bralgu. Women dance in the background.

Photo: R. Thorne, Yirrkalla, 1968.

Figure 19. This shows another aspect of the scene illustrated in Figure 18. Actors represent *mogwoi* spirits at Bralgu, the Island of the Dead to which the deceased's spirit will go. Women dance in the background.

Photo: R. Thorne, Yirrkalla, 1968.

Figure 20. This illustration shows further dancing in the same mortuary ritual. The central figure holding a fighting-bag between his teeth represents a Dreaming goanna (of the Djanggawul cycle): surrounding men are honey bees from the Woial myth-cycle.

Photo: R. Thorne, Yirrkalla, 1968.

Figure 21. This bark painting depicts the Fertility Mother, Waramurunggundji. See Fascicle Two, Chapter Four, *i* and Fascicle Three, Chapter Four continued, under Fertility Rites. Across one shoulder is slung a net bag containing lily roots, and one of her children (Nawanag) is under her left arm. She is associated with the *ubar* rituals. The artist is Maragar of the Mangeri tribe, traditionally located around Oenpelli, in western Arnhem Land. The painting was obtained in 1949-50 by R. Berndt and is now in the collection at the Department of Anthropology, University of Western Australia.

Figures 22 to 26 belong to the *ubar* ritual series of bark paintings from Oenpelli, western Arnhem Land (Gunwinggu tribe): see Fascicle Two, Chapter Four, *ii*.

Figure 22. This illustration shows two men representing red-eyed *jawul* pigeons: they wear cockatoo feathers on their heads, and the decoration on their bodies is of the x-ray art style. Between them is the secret-sacred *ubar* drum or gong. This object is identified with the Fertility Mother (see Figure 21) and Ngaljod, female Rainbow Snake: it is also her uterus. The painting is by Midjaumidjau, Gunwinggu tribe. Collected by R. Berndt at Oenpelli, 1950, and now in the collection of the Department of Anthropology, University of Western Australia.

Figure 23. This figure also belongs to the *ubar* ritual series of bark paintings. The central figure is a blanket lizard actor. The *ubar* drum lies on the ground, and the actor has emerged from a clump of bushes not shown in the painting, while one man sings (using clapping-sticks) and the other plays a didjeridu. The men are decorated and have bunches of cockatoo feathers in their hair. This is called *balanara* dancing. The artist is Midjaumidjau, Gunwinggu; it was collected at Oenpelli in 1950 by R. Berndt and is now in the collection of the Department of Anthropology, University of Western Australia.

Figure 24. This too is a scene from the *ubar* rituals. The top five dancers represent the centipede, and the bottom four the long *garbara* yam. Each group belongs to a different moiety. As they dance, the actors call invocations to the mythic beings associated with their dramatization. The artist of this bark painting is Midjaumidjau (as above). It was collected in 1950 by R. Berndt and is now in the collection of the Department of Anthropology, University of Western Australia.

Figure 25. This shows a scene from the *ubar* rituals at Oenpelli. The top two men play a didjeridu and sing with clapping-sticks. In the row immediately below, from left to right, are two *gulubar* brown kangaroo men (of one moiety), followed by three *galgbed* red wallaby dancers (of the opposite moiety). In the bottom row are three more *gulubar* dancers, and the sacred shelter (bottom right) in which the *ubar* drum is hidden: in the right bottom corner are two *galgbed* dancers, one holding a dancing-wand. Artist, Midjaumidjau (as above). Collected in 1950 at Oenpelli by R. Berndt and now in the collection of the Department of Anthropology, University of Western Australia.

Figure 26. Two *ubar* ritual actors sit back to back, clasping each other's hands. They represent the *balngbalng* (or *djurul* night bird). Cane circles hanging loosely around their shoulders represent the yellow *balmadbara* tree snake. The artist is Midjaumidjau (as above). Collected in 1950 at Oenpelli by R. Berndt and now in the collection of the Department Anthropology, University of Western Australia.

Figures 27 to 32 belong to a series of cave paintings from Deaf Adder Creek, western Arnhem Land.

Figure 27. This illustration depicts a highly conventionalized representation of a female with bird head and snake-like body, and two male figures, back to back: the penis of one is visible. It is probably a female Rainbow Snake, Ngaljod—see Figure 22, and Fascicle Two, Chapter Four, *ii* and Fascicle Three, Chapter Four continued, under Fertility Rites. Beneath the penis is a small horned Rainbow Snake. The figures are 55 inches across, on a white ochre base with red-ochre lines. They are located on the ceiling of a shelter, above a pool of water, Site 49.

Photo: E. Brandl, 1968-69.

Figure 28. This example shows *mimi*-like spirits round a large snake. The scene resembles the mythical killing of a Ngaljod Rainbow Snake in its manifestation as a 'bad' Mother: see R. and C. Berndt, *Man, Land and Myth in North Australia. The Gunwinggu People*, Sydney 1970. E. Brandl, who photographed this in 1968-69, comments that these are bi-sexual human and two small kangaroo-like creatures and the snake is Jingana, the 'Mother' who is both male and female, according to Rembranga informants at Bamyili settlement. This creature is said to have 'grown' two eggs and given birth to a daughter named Ngalgunburijaimi (of fish-like shape) and a son named Borlung (who looked like a snake). It was later identified by a Ngalgbon man as Jingana, and the two small creatures as the son and daughter.

Such paintings are of considerable age. Living Aborigines do not always know their meanings, and interpret them according to current mythology. My own interpretation would favour the Ngaljod-Jingana; the surrounding men are not necessarily bi-sexual. It also seems that their hair could be standing on end in fear: they hold clubs rather than boomerangs, which were not ordinarily used in this area, although they may have been at an earlier period.

Painted in brown-red lines (red-ochre mixed with blood?), it is located on the ceiling of a small shelter, Site 42: length of snake from head to tip of tail, 11 inches.

Photo: E. Brandl.

Figure 29. A female figure resembling a Ngaljod Rainbow Snake superimposed on older paintings. Its colouring is a faded red, and it is located in a three-foot-high shelter under a boulder at Site 27, Kolondjorluk: length, from top to bottom of painting, 34 inches.

Photo: E. Brandl, 1968-69.

Figure 30. Representation of a yam, probably for increase purposes. The tails of larger paintings of kangaroos pass across the yam. There is also a number of smaller unidentified figures. It is located on the ceiling of a ten-foot-high shelter under a boulder at Site 27, Kolondjorluk. Full length of painting, in dark brown and red colouring, is 39 inches.

Photo: E. Brandl, 1968-69.

Figure 31. Unidentified painting, possibly of a bird. Same location as paintings in figures 29 and 30. Full length, 3 to 4 feet, of dark colour.

Photo: E. Brandl, 1968-69.

Figure 32. Central figure of yam (about 30 inches in length), below a long-necked tortoise and a kangaroo (upper right-hand corner), among other paintings. Colour, faded brown to red. These are located on the underside of a projecting rock, about 15 feet from the ground, at Site 27, Kolondjorluk.

Photo: E. Brandl, 1968-69.

Figures 33 to 39 constitute a series relevant to the Lake Eyre Basin of South Australia (see this Fascicle, One, Chapter Two, 1). They are unannotated, and come from the George Aiston collection at the South Australian Museum. My own descriptions of these rest *a* on G. Horne and G. Aiston (*ibid.*) and *b* on my own knowledge of Dieri ritual life. The negatives from which these prints were made are held by the South Australian Museum. Their actual date is uncertain, but must have been prior to 1924. It would seem likely that this particular *mindari* (shown in Figures 33 to 38) took place at Mungeranie bore, south of Lake Howitt in Wonggangura tribal territory, and the incoming group were from Cowarie station on the Warburton, west of Lake Howitt.

Figure 33. Men prepare for the *mindari* in their windbreak on the secret-sacred ground.

Figure 34. Men stand in their windbreak wearing full *mindari* decoration. Aiston writes that two groups, the Red Ochre Party and the Mulyeroo, Mud Group, are involved: those depicted here are the latter. Their body designs have been made with powdered gypsum, and the bands by scraping finger nails down the arms, back and chest. On their heads are nets stuffed with emu feathers—since the *mindari* is associated with the Emu *mura* (Dreaming)—and topped by bunches of cockatoo feathers. They wear white headbands and long tassels of white rabbit fur. They have, also, cross-shoulder-belts of twisted fibre, ochred, with emu feathers stuck in the back.

Figure 35. As for Figure 34: a closer view of the decorated *mindari* participants.

Figure 36. As for Figures 34 and 35. The *mindari* group move toward the dancing ground.

Figure 37. A group of women decorated for the *mindari*: some wear nose bones.

Figure 38. Behind the bough screen on the *mindari* ground: men decorate themselves with eagle-down stuck on with fat and whitened with gypsum: down their chests is a band of charcoal, which heightens the white colouring. These designs represent a *muramura* being (unidentified) who travelled through Wonggangura territory. The women shown in Figure 37 have danced at the other side of the screen.

Figure 39. The actor in this plate is performing a rain-making ritual associated with the Rain *muramura*. His shoulders are decorated with a paste made of powdered red-ochre and blood on which white down has been stuck. A net bag full of white down has been pulled over his hair and, projecting from his head, a hoop of thin root (covered with blood and ochre) proclaims his invisibility, as a native doctor. In his hands he holds a wooden dish containing water mixed with 'rain stone' (clear gypsum). As a group of men sing (not shown), he swishes water from his dish in each direction with a bunch of eagle feathers, making the sound of rain falling. The Rain *mura* this actor depicts is associated with Mungeranie waterhole.

Figures 40 to 41 are reproductions of old paintings appearing in G. F. Angas (*ibid.*). Ceremonial and ritual material for the lower River Murray in South Australia is extremely rare. See this Facsicle, Chapter Two, 2.

Figure 40. The dancing depicted was called *guri*, held on moonlight nights when members of several tribes met (that is, of the Narinyeri constellation). Before seated men and women, a group is shown dancing: it is led by a man holding a *wanigi*-like object tipped with bunches of feathers. According to Angas, this was called *palyertatta*, and made of possum fur twine. Behind his back another dancer holds a towering emblem, which is a long spear with a bunch of feathers at its apex: human hair is wound down the whole length of the object, which is probably a conventionalized representation of a mythic being. Gum leaves bunched together are attached to the actors' knees, making a rustling sound as they dance: their bodies are painted in white ochre. Angas remarks that this form of dancing was more frequent among the Aborigines to the north of Adelaide (in South Australia), and this is suggested by the presence of the *wanigi*.

Figure 41. This is a typical example of lower River Murray dancing. A small group of women sit beating on a possum skin drum or clap two sticks together. The dance is called *palli*. The actors are painted 'like skeletons', and are arranged in rows. They dance, shaking their legs, and end each section with a call. At intervals they rush toward the women, clashing their spears together over their heads. It is probable that this was a mortuary or death ritual, since the designs on the actors approximate those that were painted on a corpse placed on a platform for smoke drying.

Figures 42 to 56 make up a series of *bora* ritual scenes, and were obtained from the booksellers Tyrrell's of Sydney. All are marked as having been photographed by Kerry of Sydney, were taken on old glass plates, and are undated: no locations are given, and at the bottom of each photograph is a brief annotation. In the following descriptions I note these latter, but interpret in my own terms. The locations were probably within the Sydney area, but may refer to several areas in New South Wales and Victoria. The dates would possibly fall within the last quarter of the 19th. century although they could be later. See this Fascicle, Chapter Two, 3.

Figure 42. This is entitled 'the sick warrior'. However, it is obvious that a novice is being shown the grooved patterning made in the sand of the *bora* ground. This probably represents the travels of a mythic being. The novice is partially covered by a blanket and is held by a guardian.

Figure 43. This is entitled 'approaching the king's ground'. However, here again, covered novices are being led by their guardians down the *bora* ground, on which grooved patterns have been made in the sand: these refer to myths. In the background is a 'nest' in a tree, used as a repository for sacred objects or as a symbolic nest in a ritual act.

Figure 44. This is entitled 'crossing the mystic figure'. However, a blanketed novice is being taken by his guardian across the grooved patterning in the sand on the *bora* ground. Behind him another novice awaits his turn, while participants surround them making an archway of spears. These are probably symbolic tracks leading to the figure in the foreground which could be a conventionalized figure of Daramulun.

Figure 45. This is entitled 'opening the *bora*'. This probably shows participants entering the *bora* ground for ritual. Around the ground patterning are mounds shown also in Figures 47, 48 *et seq.*

Figure 46. This illustration is entitled 'death of the deity'. However, this is an earth figure built up on a basis of logs and brush and covered with sand, and probably representing Baiami and/or Daramulun. Surrounding participants make an archway of boomerangs, the ritual leader standing on the figure.

Figure 47. This is entitled 'arrival of the king'. However, this is a section of a ritual act on the *bora* ground. The grooved patterning is fringed with participants; at the head are two ritual leaders, probably in readiness for singing; behind them can be seen the mounds of earth which are an extension of the *bora* ground.

Figure 48. This is entitled 'lying in wait'. Here again this shows the long track of grooved designs made on the *bora* ground. On the right is a row of mounds in which boughs have been set up: among these, participants await the coming of novices.

Figure 49. This is entitled 'spearing the wild bull'. Among the mounds on which boughs have been erected are further grooved sand designs, among them a naturalistic figure of a bull. From the actions of the two participants, this could be interpreted as symbolic spearing—hunting magic. More likely, it represents a dramatized act with singing referring to the increase of that species (which in this case, the bull, is not indigenous to Australia).

Figure 50. This is entitled 'gathering wild birds' eggs'. It probably shows an increase rite: the mounds over which the four men are bent represent nests and from these they remove eggs. The ritual leader (left), himself bent, is holding an egg in one hand: he is probably chanting or singing. In the background are onlookers, among them three novices who are now permitted to witness this rite.

Figure 51. This is entitled 'the *bora* tree'. The ground designs on the *bora* ground are seen to lead to or from the tree a participant is climbing. Branches are set up on the mounds and in the foreground is a 'nest' with stones in it. The tree itself has deep grooves, two of which resemble 'hands'. This is probably a conventionalized representation of Baiami-Daramulun.

Figure 52. This is entitled 'waiting the decision of the kings'. In this example of *bora* ritual, two men stand on specially built mounds, surrounded by a shallow trench: they hold conventional weapons, and in each mound weapons are stuck. Before the sitting group of covered novices and their guardians, the ritual leader stands on a special platform or tree stump, holding a club. Behind is a windbreak.

Figure 53. This is entitled 'a duel to the death', but is in fact part of the ritual shown in Figure 52. It is probably associated with the testing of novices as part of the initiatory sequence. The glass plate is severely damaged.

Figure 54. This is entitled 'spearing the alligator'. However, this act belongs to the increase series of *bora* rituals, and the grooved figure in the sand is that of a kangaroo. Men symbolically spear this.

Figure 55. This is entitled 'following the footsteps of the deity'. Men move down the *bora* ground, probably re-telling (or chanting) a particular incident in the life of a mythic being, concerning the grooved ground figure of an emu. A spear shaft is in the bird and the leader is pointing at it: small track-like depressions (the second man on the right is pointing at one) are probably the footprints of Daramulun. Emu was regarded as the wife of Baiami/Daramulun.

Figure 56. This is entitled 'death of the wild boar'. In a rite probably of increase intent, a man is shown symbolically spearing a wild pig (non-indigenous species). Another man is poised over a 'nest' mound: see Figure 50.

PLATES AND MAPS

1. Painting a *djuwei* post for a *djunggawon* circumcision ritual. Elcho Island, Arnhem Land.

2. Two *djuwei* posts being prepared for a *djunggawon* circumcision ritual.
Elcho Island, Arnhem Land.

3. Men working on ritual objects. Elcho Island, Arnhem Land.

4. *Jiridja* moiety mortuary dancing. Yirrkalla, Arnhem Land.

5. Wuramu mortuary figure. Elcho Island, Arnhem Land.

6. Sacred patterns on a canoe. Yirrkalla, Arnhem Land.

8. Wooden image of the younger Wawalag
Sister. Yirrkalla, Arnhem Land.

7. *Djuwei* post representing the elder Wawalag Sister.
Elcho Island, Arnhem Land.

10. Wooden image of Kultana, spirit guardian in *jiridja* moiety Land of the Dead. Yirrkalla, Arnhem Land.

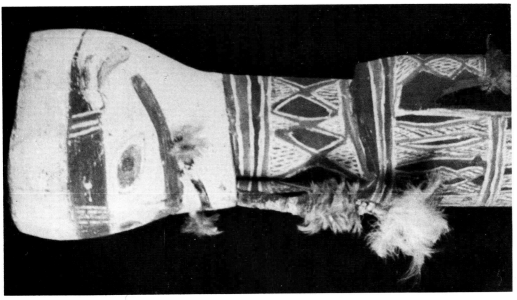

9. Wooden image of Laindjung. Yirrkalla, Arnhem Land.

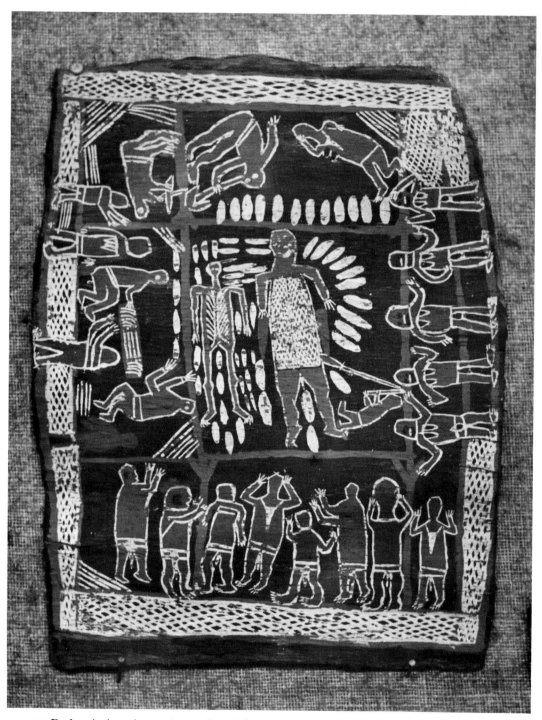

11. Bark painting of a mortuary rite, at the mortuary platform. Yirrkalla, Arnhem Land.

12. Bark painting of a sacred pattern, Gumaidj dialect unit. Yirrkalla, Arnhem Land.

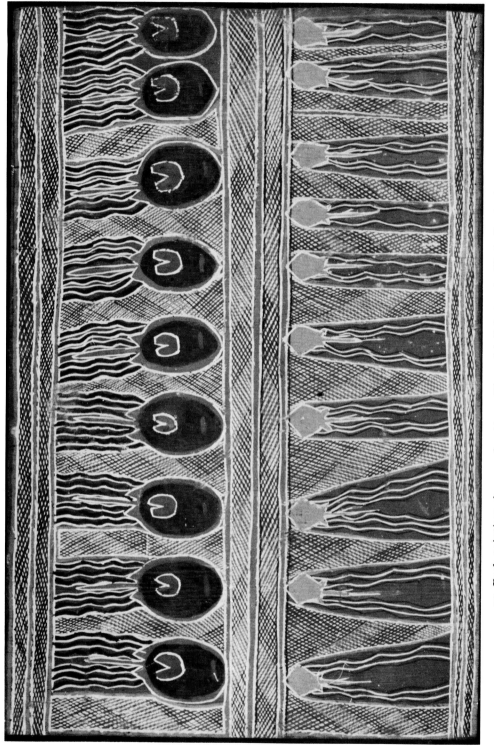

13. Bark painting of a sacred pattern, Waramiri dialect unit. Yirrkalla, Arnhem Land.

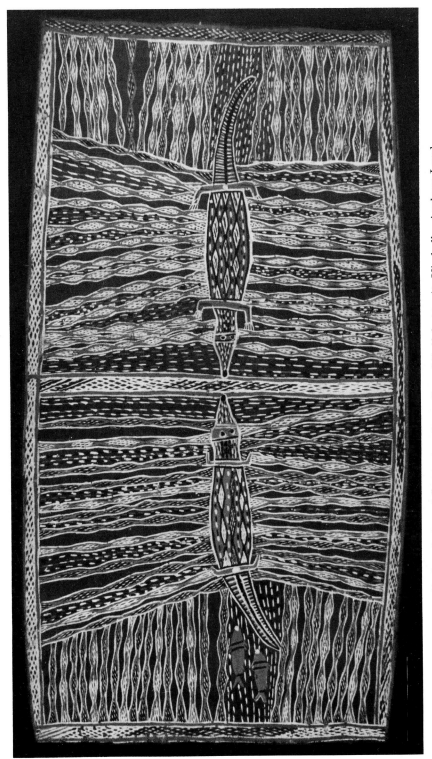

14. Bark painting of a sacred pattern, Gumaidj dialect unit. Yirrkalla, Arnhem Land.

15. Yirrkalla, delayed mortuary ritual: typical decoration on the chief mourner, the dead man's son.

16. Yirrkalla, delayed mortuary ritual: ritual goanna posturing, associated with the Djanggawul mythic beings.

17. Yirrkalla, delayed mortuary ritual: *rangga* emblems of non-secret variety associated with the mythic Wawalag Sisters.

18. Yirrkalla, delayed mortuary ritual: dancers representing *mogwoi* spirits in *dua* moiety Land of the Dead.

19. Yirrkalla, delayed mortuary ritual: dancers representing *mogwoi* spirits.

20. Yirrkalla, delayed mortuary ritual: central dancer represents Dreaming goanna.

21. Bark painting of Fertility Mother, Waramurunggundji. Oenpelli, Arnhem Land.

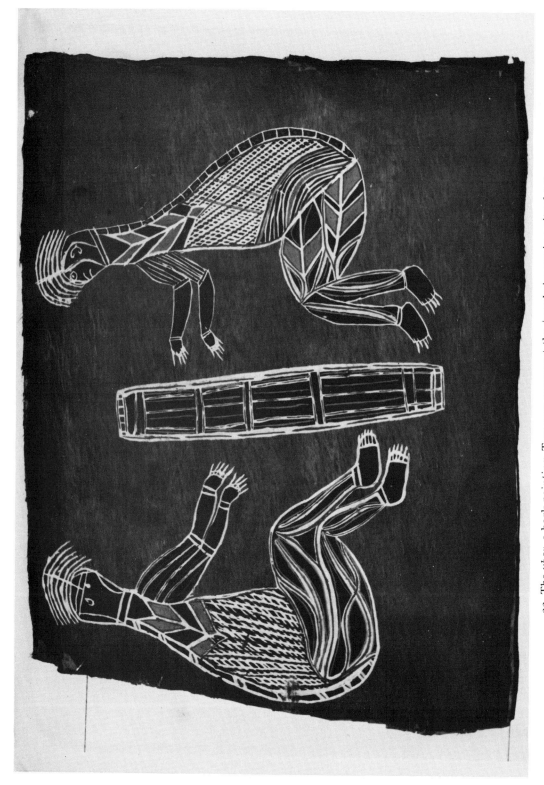

22. The *ubar*, a bark painting. Two men represent the *jawul* pigeons in a ritual act. Oenpelli, Arnhem Land.

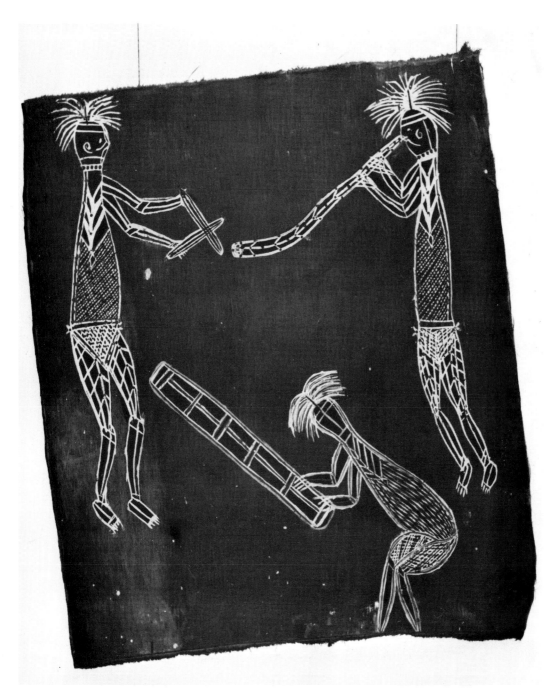

23. The *ubar*, a bark painting. Ritual performance with the *ubar* drum, accompanied by the singing man and didjeridu player. Oenpelli, Arnhem Land.

24. The *ubar*, a bark painting. Centipede and Yam ritual dancers. Oenpelli, Arnhem Land.

25. The *ubar*, a bark painting. Brown Kangaroo and red Wallaby ritual dancers. Oenpelli, Arnhem Land.

26. The *ubar*, a bark painting. Balngbalng night bird ritual dancers. Oenpelli, Arnhem Land.

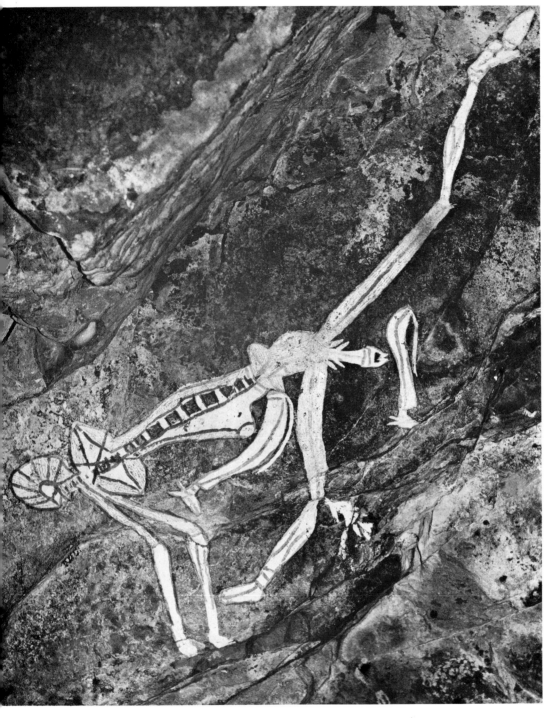

27. Cave painting: probably of the Rainbow Snake, Ngaljod. Deaf Adder Creek, Arnhem Land.

28. Cave painting: probably of the Rainbow Snake (main figure), surrounded by smaller human figures.
Deaf Adder Creek Arnhem Land

29. Cave painting: main figure, probably of the Rainbow Snake.
Deaf Adder Creek, Arnhem Land.

30. Cave painting: yam, probably for increase purposes. Deaf Adder Creek, Arnhem Land.

31. Cave painting: probably of a bird. Deaf Adder Creek, Arnhem Land.

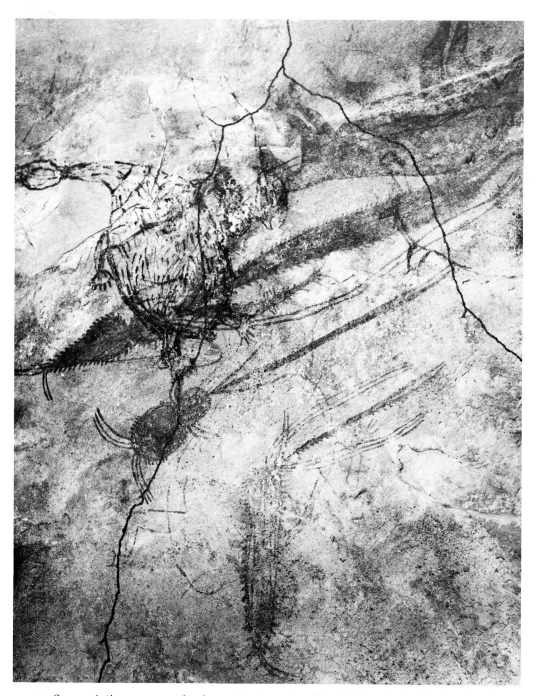

32. Cave painting: yam, and other natural species. Deaf Adder Creek, Arnhem Land.

33. Lake Eyre Basin: preparing for *mindari* ritual.

34. Lake Eyre Basin: men decorated for the *mindari* ritual.

35. Lake Eyre Basin: decorated *mindari* participants.

36. Lake Eyre Basin: a *mindari* group

37. Lake Eyre Basin: women decorated for the *mindari*.

38. Lake Eyre Basin: men decorating for the *mindari*
behind their bough screen.

39. Lake Eyre Basin: Rain Dreaming ritual.

40. Lower River Murray: a *guri* dance.

41. Lower River Murray: a *palti* dance.

42. *Bora* ritual: novice being shown sacred grooved pattern in sand.

43. *Bora* ritual: covered novices led by guardians down the secret-sacred ground.

44. *Bora* ritual: novice with his guardian, led under an archway of spears, crosses the mythic track leading to Daramulun.

45. *Bora* ritual: entering the secret-sacred ground.

46. *Bora* ritual: an earth figure of Daramulun. Men surround it forming an archway of boomerangs.

47. *Bora* ritual: a ritual act before the grooved patterning, with two leaders.

48. *Bora* ritual: the grooved designs in the sand. Postulants hide behind boughs which have been set up on a series of mounds.

49. *Bora* ritual: symbolic spearing of a bull.

50. *Bora* ritual: increase ritual relevant to eggs. The mounds symbolize nests.

51. *Bora* ritual: climbing a *bora* tree sacred to Daramulun. Before the tree are the grooved designs and mounds.

52. *Bora* ritual: posturing on mounds, with weapons, before covered novices and their guardians.

53. *Bora* ritual: testing of novices.

54. *Bora* ritual: symbolic spearing of a kangaroo.

55. *Bora* ritual: symbolic spearing of an emu.

56. *Bora* ritual: symbolic spearing of a wild pig.